LANDS and PEOPLES

SPECIAL EDITION:
UPHEAVAL IN EUROPE

GROLIER

LANDS and PEOPLES

SPECIAL EDITION:
UPHEAVAL IN EUROPE

STAFF

Lawrence T. Lorimer ....Editorial Director
Joseph M. Castagno ....Executive Editor
Irina Rybacek ....Text Author
Doris E. Lechner........................Managing Editor
Tone Imset Ruccio ....Art Director
David M. Buskus ....Copy Editor
Elizabeth Farrington ....Art Assistant
Ann Eriksen ....Chief, Photo Research
Pauline M. Sholtys ....,......Chief Indexer
Joseph J. Corlett ....Director of Manufacturing
Christine L. Matta .....Senior Production Manager
Barbara L. Persan ....Production Manager
Pamela J. Murphy................Production Assistant

ISBN 0-7172-8014-4

Printed in the United States of America

Contents

One of the most dramatic events of the century occurred in November 1989, when East German authorities opened the Berlin Wall, for years a vivid symbol of Communist oppression.

UPHEAVAL IN EUROPE:
The Gathering Storm

In the spring of 1989, very few people had a sense of an approaching drama in Eastern Europe. Soviet perestroika was in its fourth year, and after the defeat of hard-line candidates in the March elections to the Congress of People's Deputies, many observers both inside the U.S.S.R. and in the West felt a cautious optimism that a transformation of the Soviet system was indeed possible. In Poland, the banned trade union Solidarity was being readmitted into the official political arena, but since Solidarity had never really ceased to exist, its formal reemergence was not that surprising. In Hungary, the disintegration of Communist authority proceeded calmly, step-by-step. Yugoslavia occasionally appeared in the news as a country with ethnic problems, but that was nothing new, either. The rest of Eastern Europe—East Germany, Czechoslovakia, Romania, Bulgaria, and Albania—was (or rather, seemed to be) firmly in the grip of Communist conservatives determined to withstand any challenge to their power. A few demonstrations in Prague, Czechoslovakia, were briskly and efficiently suppressed. And so it appeared that everything would go on as usual for quite some time.

But although the upheaval in Eastern Europe came as a surprise to most people, it was in fact not surprising. If you had peered under the calm surface of the hard-line Communist regimes, you could have seen that their societies were sick and getting sicker every day: declining economy, diseased environment, cynicism, feelings of hopelessness, desperation, and dead end. Most of the popular support that Communist regimes had enjoyed during their four decades of existence had already evaporated by the spring of 1989, and the only prop that held them in place was the mighty Soviet Union. Ironically, however, the Soviet system itself was now being undermined by Mikhail Gorbachev.

It would be interesting to know whether the Hungarian officials who ordered the Hungarian-Austrian border to be opened in early May 1989 had a foreboding that this breaching of the Iron Curtain would quickly lead to the collapse of Communist regimes throughout Eastern Europe. Whatever they thought, this event was the beginning of a few dramatic months that changed the face of Europe and the world.

This book is a multilayered portrayal of what happened in late 1989, an effort to explain why it happened, and a look into the future. In the following pages of this introductory section, we will go back in time to look at the origins of Communism and socialism and to review briefly the tortured history of this movement throughout the 20th century. The next section of the Introduction will discuss the main features of Communist regimes, and the section after that will deal with daily life in Communist countries, including such matters as shopping, cultural life, political humor, and religion. The Introduction will close with a consideration of the main social groups that have pushed for political changes during the decades of Communist rule.

The second part of the book is a chronology, which traces the developments in Eastern Europe from 1944 onward, and is organized in columns, country by country. Until the late 1980s, only the most crucial events are listed, but for the past three years, the chronology goes month by month.

Names and terms appearing in the chronology in boldface are the main entries in the third part of the book, the alphabetical section. Approximately 100 entries include all the Eastern European countries, some important regions, all the individual republics of the U.S.S.R., the most important protagonists, and some terms and organizations. The entries are brief and in some cases are just quick overviews, but we have tried always to pinpoint the crucial characteristics of a country, a person, or a term.

The book concludes with a brief consideration of the future: "Looking Toward the Next Century." One year after the upheaval, it has become quite clear that the toppling of Communist rulers was an easy matter

Between the world wars, several new democracies emerged in Eastern Europe.

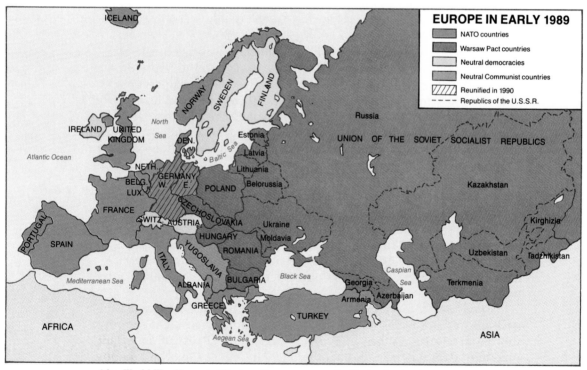

After World War II, most of Eastern Europe came under Soviet domination.

once their main prop, the U.S.S.R., refused to support them anymore; but the true change from totalitarian regimes into democratic ones will be an arduous, long, and complex task.

Historical Background

Origins of Socialism and Communism. Communist regimes have caused so much suffering in so many parts of the world that all other tyrannies throughout the whole of human history pale in comparison. And yet this greatest modern tragedy started with a dream. The words "socialism" and "Communism," dating from the 1830s and 1840s, stood for a vision of a new and better world, without social and economic injustice and inequality, in which all the means of production would belong to the whole community. Despite continuing disputes whether Marx, Lenin, and other founding fathers of this movement were visionaries or power seekers, it is a fact that millions of people in many parts of the world believed, some for a short time and others for their whole lives, that socialism and Communism are the noblest goals of human history and a cause worth dying for.

In the middle of the 19th century, German thinker and revolutionary Karl Marx formulated a theory of Communism as the highest stage in history, in which all exploitation and poverty would be abolished, people would work in creative ways, and the state with its powers of repression would vanish. Marx then predicted the coming of a world revolution that would usher in socialism—as a transitory stage between capitalism and Communism—and the "dictatorship of the proletariat." Marx's theory underwent multiple metamorphoses, and its promise of equality and justice has proved extremely vital for more than a hundred years.

The Rise of the Soviet Union. When Lenin formed his Bolshevik Party (which became the Communist Party after the October Revolution in 1917), he complemented the original Marxist vision with an important new addition: he made the party the leader of society. Lenin died a few years after the Communists took power, and students of Soviet history still argue whether or not the Soviet regime would have become more benevolent under his leadership or not. The fact remains that Lenin's successor, Stalin, created such a malign, evil, and oppressive system that it does not have an equal in the whole of human history. The reasons for this are complex and include both Stalin's personality and the legacies of Russian history: Stalin was a man who yearned to be the ultimate ruler, suspicious of everyone, probably full of inferiority complexes, which he compensated by getting rid of all his real and potential adversaries, and certainly paranoid in his later years; and at the same time very devious and scheming, able to deceive not only his compatriots but many Westerners as well. Russian history and society were another important part of the equation: when the Bolsheviks took over, most of the population were illiterate peasants, for whom the words "democracy" and "freedom" smacked of "anarchy." When these two ingredients, Stalin and Russia, combined with a theory of state ownership of all means of production and the leading role of the party, the result was the monstrous Stalinist socialism.

Communist Expansion Throughout the World. At a tremendous cost in human lives and with an almost unimaginable waste, Stalin managed to transform the Soviet Union from a feudal backward empire into an industrialized mammoth. In 1945, by means of the Yalta agreements with Western Allied powers, he then laid ground for the post-World War II expansion. As the Soviet armies advanced west, pursuing German troops, the future Communist territory was carved out. Ever suspicious of the West, from 1944 onward Stalin went on systematically engineering and promoting Communist takeovers in Eastern Europe. The mechanism of these takeovers was similar: Communist parties first allied with other parties, then gradually weakened them, subverted or co-opted them, and finally usurped all power. Some Eastern European Communist governments were directly imposed by the Soviet armies (in Bulgaria or Romania, for instance), and others emerged after a few years, for instance in Czechoslovakia. Two exceptions to the crucial role of the U.S.S.R. were Yugoslavia and Albania, where strong national leaders appeared during the war: both Tito and Hoxha were guerrilla heroes and commanded genuine respect among the population.

The first period of Communism in Eastern Europe was a somewhat diluted copy of the Stalinist 1930s: expropriation of private property, nationalizations, collectivization of agriculture, abolition of civil liberties, purges of anti-Communist opposition and persecution of "class enemies," show trials, executions, and widespread terror. After these harsh years, Eastern Europe settled into a more lenient stage, which was less explicitly brutal, but in many ways more pernicious.

Meanwhile, Communist regimes arose also in Asia. The second-oldest Communist country in the world is Mongolia, which became a "People's Republic" in November 1924. After World War II, China and North Korea joined the Communist world, and, in 1954, North Vietnam followed suit. And so, in the mid-20th century, the largest country in the world, the most populous country in the world, and a score of others were dominated by Communists, and it seemed that Communism was indeed marching toward victory.

The Main Characteristics of Communist Societies

The Leading Role of the Party. This was the main contribution of Lenin to the old Marxist theory: the party is the vanguard of the proletariat, the leader of the whole society. All ruling Communist parties (very often called by different names, without the word "Communist") had a constitutional monopoly on power. The first rule in George Orwell's *Animal Farm* was: "All animals are equal, but some are more equal," and this axiom precisely describes the situation in the Communist countries: party members were more equal. From top to bottom of society, party members were the bosses: there were party cells in each village, in each school, in each factory, in each army unit, and these cells made the real decisions about everything—from the "correct party line" concerning some regional conflict at the other side of the world, to the handling of young people with long hair and a love for Western music. One can visualize the party as a huge pyramid, with directives coming from the top down to the lowest levels.

The party and the state were intertwined, but the party was decisive. In Bulgaria, Czechoslovakia, East Germany, Hungary before 1956, and Poland, there were other "shadow" political parties, but they were totally dependent on the Communists—they could not recruit new members, and at their congresses they regularly expressed their full support for

Much of Eastern Europe lay in ruins following World War II.

Communist policies. They were just a "window dressing" in the game of democracy.

Another element in this "let's pretend" game was the elections, an important regular Communist ritual that was supposed to prove that the ruling parties—which proclaimed themselves to be the parties of the working class—enjoyed the full support of the people. But there was no election, no choice, because there was just one candidate for each position. Every citizen was obliged to participate, and the results were always just below 100 percent—99.55 percent or a similar figure, allowing for a few insignificant individuals to disagree with the "party line."

The persons occupying high party and state positions were collectively known as the nomenclature, a rather closed group of insiders who ruled the country. The nomenclature included all top party bosses, government ministers, chairmen of important state agencies, directors of large industrial enterprises and banks, and high army officers. A crucial part of the nomenclature was the secret police. Known as *KGB* in the Soviet Union, *Sigurimi* in Albania, *Securitate* in Romania, and *Stasi* in East Germany, the secret police was a powerful force in all of Eastern Europe, but there were differences between individual countries, ranging from the almost total grip on society by the Albanian and Romanian varieties, to the somewhat more liberal Hungarian and Polish versions. Tens of thousands of people were helping the police as informers (*Stasi*, for instance, had 85,000 full-time agents and over 500,000 part-time informers).

The Ruling Ideology of Marxism-Leninism. In its most simplistic form, Marxism-Leninism was a set of formulas and pronouncements that, by being endlessly repeated, were at least partially accepted by a great number of people. "All history until the advent of socialism was marked by class struggle between the oppressors and the oppressed" was one such formula; others ranged from a condemnation of profit making as antisocial, to the notion that the party is the protector of the working people, and to the praises of the Soviet Union as the "cradle of socialism." Another theme endlessly repeated was the sacrifices undergone by Communists in the struggle against Nazism. From kindergarten to university, students had to take classes in Marxism-Leninism, and learn by rote the various dogmas. The enforcement of this systematic brainwashing varied in time and by country: the indoctrination became extremely perfunctory in the last decades in Poland or in Hungary; but in the conservative regimes such as Romania or Bulgaria, no one dared to challenge the official preaching ideology; and in "normalized" Czechoslovakia, almost everyone paid lip service to it even though no one believed in it any longer.

In the early period of the Communist era, Marxism-Leninism was a sort of religion for many people. A believing Communist often resembled a member of a dogmatic religious sect with whom you can talk for hours, and who always counters your objections and criticism with a ready argument. But as it became increasingly clear to an ever greater number of people that the Communist system did not work and that the Communist countries would not only not surpass the capitalist world (as Khrushchev boasted in the late 1950s), but that they were lagging behind in every possible aspect, Marxism-Leninism turned into a hollow incan-

Soviet tanks propped up the Communist regimes imposed on postwar Eastern Europe.

For decades, Communist government bodies simply rubber-stamped the decisions of the Party elite.

tation of phrases. It is very probable that when Ceauşescu talked about the "radiant summits of Communism" in December 1987, most of the undernourished, freezing Romanian population did not believe him.

Command Economy. Command economy, or centrally planned economy, or Marxist economy, was for decades hailed as the true "scientific" way to direct the economic life of a society. It has by now become obvious that command economy brought economic ruin to all countries where it had been implemented. It had several basic characteristics:

• Central Planning: Economic decisions were made by huge bureaucracies. Individual entrepreneurship, initiative, and industriousness were not only unwelcome, but were often punished by demotion, harassment, or other means.

• Price Controls: All prices were set by the state agencies and often remained unchanged for years.

• State as the Major Employer: The state sector was by far the largest one, and so most of the population worked for the state. There was no unemployment, and to fire a person for incompetence was so difficult that it almost never happened (people could easily be fired for political reasons, however). Because salaries were uniformly low, there was no incentive to work hard, and a typical person, whether a blue- or a white-collar worker, worked as little as possible.

• Emphasis on Heavy Industry: This went back to Stalin and to his preference for huge industrial complexes. All Eastern European regimes concentrated on this sector, and so, for instance, Czechoslovakia came to produce 15 million tons of steel every year (1 ton per person), and one Romanian superfactory used more electricity than all the private homes throughout the country. Most of these mammoth enterprises were superbly inefficient.

• Neglect of Services and Chronic Shortages: This was the other side of the coin of heavy industrialization. Not only were there not enough stores, repair shops, restaurants, and other services, but those that exist-

9

ed were poorly supplied. The shortages varied country by country, from the lack of basic foodstuffs in Romania to occasional shortages of particular items in Czechoslovakia or Hungary (one summer there was no garlic; half a year later, there was no toilet paper; and so on).

• Undeveloped Banking System: Virtually everything was paid in cash: salaries, wages, and all purchases. When you paid your rent and utilities, you had to go to a post office and send a money order. People were not used to buying on installment plans, and there were no credit cards (but Western credit cards were accepted in major cities).

• "Shadow Economy" and Black Market were a necessary complement of the malfunctioning official economic system. Almost everyone stole from the state, and some items, such as building materials (cement, bricks, wood) were often stolen on a grand scale. Because it was so hard to get goods and services, there was a widespread "barter economy" and a network of "connections": someone fixed your broken TV set, and you supplied him in return with black-market hard currency; or another person got you a high-quality cut of beef, and you repaid with a bottle of Western perfume.

There were great economic differences between individual Communist countries, with East Germany generally considered to be relatively well-off, and Romania and Bulgaria taking the last places. But it was only during 1990 that the true extent of Communist economic mismanagement began to be revealed, and it came as a shock to many when it turned out that even the "rational" and "efficient" East German economy was in catastrophic shape.

Agriculture has remained pitifully backward throughout much of Eastern Europe.

Education, child care (above), and medical care, though free, do not meet Western standards.

Daily Life in Communist Societies

After the initial times of terror, most Eastern European countries went through several stages, in which liberalization years alternated with more oppressive periods. Generally, however, most people had several basic certainties: they knew that unless they provoked the authorities with some political protest or even indiscretion, they would never lose their jobs. They knew that the basic foodstuffs would cost the same in years to come (in most countries, prices of bread, butter, milk, and similar items did not change for decades). They knew that they would get free education and free medical care, even if very often of substandard quality, and they could count on retirement pensions at a relatively early age, most often at the age of 55 for women and 60 for men.

The other certainties were the daily, constant frustrations. Just to provide for basic needs like food and clothing required enormous energy: standing in lines every day; going from store to store in search of scarce items, arguing with grumpy salespeople, and then carrying the heavy bags home; pushing in overcrowded streetcars or buses; on the streets, trying not to fall into gaping excavations that stayed unfinished for months. And when you got home, you found out that the water was out, or the electricity had been shut off, or your refrigerator had stopped working. To get a plumber or repairman for your appliances could take weeks unless you had the right "connections."

At work, people were generally overburdened with dozens of forms to fill out for everything, and with unreliability and inefficiency everywhere: nonworking telephones, constant delays in deliveries, nonsensical orders from above. At the same time, it was considered perfectly normal to go shopping during working hours or to a hairdresser—and to steal. "Whoever does not steal from the state, steals from his family" was a fitting expression of the attitude of many people toward "state property." Ironically, some passages in Marx's early writing dealing with work conditions in the glorious future of Communism seem to describe the current practices in industrialized countries: concern for safety, clean and well-lighted working places, efforts to make the work interesting and creative for each individual. The Communist bosses, however, couldn't care less, and so the workplaces in countries ruled by the "vanguard of the working class" were more often than not dirty, uncomfortable, unpleasant, and unsafe.

Another characteristic feature of Communist societies was the quantity of prohibitions and restrictions that you had to deal with all the time. "In the West, anything that is not expressly forbidden is permitted; while under Communism, anything that is not explicitly permitted is forbidden," said one popular joke. In the U.S.S.R., you not only could not freely travel abroad, but you had to have an *internal passport* to travel within the country. If you wanted to move or change jobs, you had to obtain multiple permissions. If you wanted to remodel your apartment, to install a gas heating system, to get a fishing license, or to apply to a university, you had to fill out endless questionnaires and to obtain approval stamps from countless agencies. If you felt sick with a flu or a cold, you could not stay home for a day or two: you had to go to your assigned doctor, wait there sometimes for hours, and then get his or her permission not to go to work. Travel was another problem, especially for the travel-eager Central Europeans. They could travel within Eastern Europe, but to get to the West was much more complicated, particularly for East Germans, who resented the restrictions very much. In the Balkan Communist countries, with the exception of Yugoslavia, travel to the West was not permitted at all.

To add insult to injury, the Communist mass media continued to extol the virtues of socialism and to condemn the evils of the West. Communist newspapers were not supposed to inform, but to carry out political propaganda, and so were full of long articles praising various accomplishments of socialism, reprints of endless boring speeches by Communist dignitaries, Central Committee resolutions, or diatribes against "antisocialist forces," "imperialist powers," or "hostile military-industrial circles." The favorite approach was not outright lying, but distortion of truth, by quoting a person out of context, by pointing only to negative features and never mentioning the positive ones, by omitting the crucial facts and stressing some secondary circumstance. Even in relatively liberal periods, for instance in Hungary during the recent decade, there were many taboos: and so the 1956 uprising was officially, until early 1989, a "counterrevolution."

Last but not least, there was the continual, ever-present fear. Except in the most oppressive periods, it was not a fear for your life, but rather, a fear of losing your job, of having your children barred from higher education, of being denied permission to travel. It was a state of being afraid to speak up, of always lowering your voice when talking about politics in public places, of feeling your stomach tighten whenever you had any dealings with a policeman, of avoiding any political talk when speaking on the phone, and never writing anything "dangerous" in letters. In fact,

Reform-minded demonstrators always risked being arrested by uniformed or undercover police.

only some phones were bugged, but you never knew whether your phone was among them; only some letters were opened, but you never knew if yours might be among them. The powers that be were simply referred to as "they," and, in Romania, the most frightening word was a simple "she," meaning Elena Ceauşescu.

How did people cope with all these indignities? One important haven was culture, which, although restricted and under political pressure from the authorities, often provided the only refuge and sense of normality. Most Eastern Europeans are avid book readers, and, until the upheaval in 1989, books were a precious commodity; when a novel by a popular Western author was to come out, people would often stand in long lines to get it, and many books would be sold out completely within a few hours. Western movies usually came with a great delay, sometimes five to 10 years after they were made, but for that reason alone, they were considered especially valuable. Theaters were generally somewhat less subject to censorship than were movies, and, in various periods, political cabarets flourished—in Czechoslovakia in the mid-1960s, in Poland during the 1970s and 1980s, in East Germany in the 1980s. Even classical pieces were sometimes understood by audiences as having poignant messages for the present: because so much was forbidden, it was often sufficient to make a simple gesture, to say a few well-coined words, and the audience understood and became suddenly united as if sharing a secret.

Another important facet of life under Communism was tuning in to foreign broadcasts. Almost all East Germans could get West German programs on their TV sets, and this daily contrast between a Communist and a Western society gave lie to all the official statements about the glories of socialism. Two radio stations that broadcast in all Eastern European languages, Radio Free Europe and Radio Liberty, have also played an important role in the unraveling of Communist regimes, particularly during the fall of 1989, when they informed in great detail about the domino fall of one hard-liner after another.

In the Central European countries, political humor was an important means by which to keep one's sanity and mental balance. Political jokes, often quite mordant and brutal, lightened up the daily grayness and made it easier to bear the constant flow of irritations. In the more oppressive periods, it could be dangerous to tell a political joke, but even in more lenient times, you would be careful in front of whom you spoke. The jokes made fun of stupid functionaries ("Who is the most sincere politician in the world? Milos Jakes [party chief in Czechoslovakia], because he looks like an idiot, speaks like an idiot, and is an idiot."), of dumb policemen, of the Soviet Union, of all the official pretensions and lies ("What is socialism? A tortuous way from capitalism to capitalism."). When family and friends met, the newest political jokes were always a welcome part of the conversation.

And finally, there was religion. The new "scientific" ideology of Marxism-Leninism was supposed to replace the old superstitious religious teachings that, according to the official atheist propaganda, had only served the oppressors in their exploitation of the masses. Karl Marx's slogan "religion is the opium of the people" was repeated millions of times after 1917 in the U.S.S.R. and later in Eastern Europe as well, and yet, despite decades of pressure and harassment and persecution, religion has survived. There were great differences between individual countries, ranging from the fiercely antireligious Albania, which closed down all places of worship in 1967, to Poland, the second most Catholic country after Italy, where the church played a large role in social and, in recent decades, political life as well. Soviet Jews, who were in the forefront of the dissident movement, combined their religious yearnings with political activism, the Protestant church in East Germany was involved in the unofficial peace movement during the 1980s, and an underground church existed in Czechoslovakia.

The Agents of Change

Despite the general impression of immobility and lack of change, the Communist regimes in Eastern Europe were live organisms like all societies and went through numerous changes. These changes were spearheaded by several major groups.

Reform Communists. A reform Communist is a person who wants to make the socialist system more humane, while keeping all the major pillars intact; that is, while maintaining the command economy, the leading role of the party, and the ruling ideology of Marxism-Leninism. The first famous Eastern European reform Communist was Tito of Yugoslavia, who rejected Soviet patronage and embarked on his special road to socialism. He was no democrat, but he instituted a much more benevolent system in Yugoslavia than was the norm in the rest of Europe. János Kádár of Hungary started as a Soviet puppet, but soon turned into a reformist and, during his long tenure, introduced the comfortable "goulash Communism" into Hungary. Poland's Władysław Gomułka began in 1956 as a reformist, but then became gradually more rigid and ended up a hard-liner. Another well-known reformist was Alexander Dubček, the symbol of Prague Spring of 1968. In the U.S.S.R., the first reform Communist was Nikita Khrushchev, who was both Stalin's heir and Gorbachev's precursor. The most famous reform Communist is, of course, Mikhail Gorbachev.

As the revolution swept throughout Eastern Europe in late 1989, reform Communism virtually disappeared from the political scene in East Germany (which ultimately disappeared as well), Poland, Czech- oslovakia, and Hungary. In Bulgaria, the mildly reformist Mladenov took over after Zhivkov, but was deposed in the summer of 1990; and the National Salvation League in Romania, also composed of former Communists who could be labeled reformist, was being challenged by an increasingly vocal opposition throughout 1990. In Yugoslavia, reform Communism also seems to have run its course, as new non-Communist parties have begun to emerge. And so, in early 1991, the only Eastern European country still trying to reform Communism was Albania.

Workers and Students. The most restive and active workers in Eastern Europe were in Poland: their strikes and protests were the red line throughout the whole Communist period. The most glorious moment came with the formation of Solidarity in 1981, but other successes were to follow: the reemergence of Solidarity in 1989, the victory in the first partially free elections, and finally the election of the most famous work- er in the world, Lech Wałęsa, to the Polish presidency in December 1990. In other countries, there were occasional worker protests—in East Germany in 1953, in Romania in the late 1980s—but these were always quickly suppressed.

Students as a group also appeared as political actors: in 1956, they were active in the liberalization movement in Hungary before the upris- ing in October; in the fall of 1967, they protested in Czechoslovakia; in 1968, Polish students demonstrated against censorship and lack of human rights. In 1989 and 1990, students played an important role in several countries: they were the first protagonists in Czechoslovakia's "velvet revolution," they demonstrated against the holdovers from the former regime in Romania throughout 1990, and they were prominent in antigov- ernment protests in Albania.

But it was the following group that consistently represented the main challenge to the rulers.

Intellectuals. Intellectuals—mostly writers—have played an abso- lutely vital role in the history of all Communist regimes. Whenever repres- sion subsided and some room appeared for dissent or simply for more openness and creativity, intellectuals would repeatedly come to the fore, thus testifying to the tenacity of human spirit. Dozens of Soviet writers and intellectuals—including Boris Pasternak, Alexander Solzhenitsyn, and Andrei Sakharov—became known worldwide in the 1960s and 1970s; Adam Michnik and Jacek Kuron from Poland, Václav Havel and Milan Kundera from Czechoslovakia, George Konrad from Hungary, Milovan Djilas from Yugoslavia, and many less-known ones followed suit. Standing alone against the whole machinery of a powerful system, they were like little Davids challenging the towering Goliaths. The con- science of their societies, these people carried the torch of freedom, courage, and persistent struggle for human rights, despite persecution, harassment, prison or exile. Their heroic resistance finally bore fruit.

UPHEAVAL IN EUROPE: A year-by-year overview

THE SOVIET UNION	ALBANIA	BULGARIA	CZECHOSLOVAKIA	EAST GERMANY

1944-1950

The wartime alliance between the U.S.S.R. and England, France, and the **U.S.** sours and turns into the **Cold War**.

The U.S.S.R. helps establish Communist regimes in **Eastern Europe**.

In January 1949, the Council for Mutual Economic Assistance (**COMECON**) is set up.

In November 1944, a Communist government under Enver Hoxha is set up.

In 1946, Albania becomes a People's Republic.

In 1948, Albania severs relations with **Yugoslavia**.

In September 1944, Soviet troops enter the country, and the Communist Party rises to power.

In October 1946, a People's Republic of Bulgaria is proclaimed.

In May 1945, Soviet troops enter the country.

In free elections in May 1946, the Communists emerge as the strongest party, with 38% of the vote.

In February 1948, Communists take power in a bloodless coup.

In June 1948, Czechoslovakia is proclaimed a People's Democracy.

In May 1945, Germany is divided into four zones; eastern Germany comes under the Soviet rule. Berlin is divided into four sectors.

In October 1949, the German Democratic Republic is founded.

In 1950, Walter Ulbricht becomes the general secretary of the Communist Party (called German Socialist Unity Party).

1953

Stalin dies in March.

A workers' uprising in June is suppressed by the Soviet armed forces.

1955

Warsaw Pact is established in May.

▲ *Agreements made at the Yalta Conference in 1945 helped shape European history for decades to come.*

1956

In February, **Khrushchev** denounces **Stalin's** crimes in a secret speech at a party congress and initiates the **de-Stalinization** process.

In 1956, an anti-Communist ▶ uprising in Hungary was brutally suppressed by Soviet troops.

1958

1960

A split between the U.S.S.R. and China becomes public; for the next three decades, the two countries will go through long periods of tension and even open hostilities.

◀ *During his years as Soviet premier, Nikita Khrushchev tried to reform many aspects of the Communist system. He was ousted from power in 1964.*

16

HUNGARY	POLAND	ROMANIA	YUGOSLAVIA	THE WEST AND OTHER COUNTRIES	
In October 1944, Soviet troops enter the country.

During 1948-49, the Hungarian Workers' Party (Communists) gradually assumes power by breaking up other parties.

In August 1949, Hungary is proclaimed a People's Democracy. | In July 1944, Soviet troops enter the country.

In January 1947, a bloc of four parties dominated by the Communists wins elections. Subsequently, the Communists (known as the Polish United Workers' Party) assume full power. | In August 1944, Soviet troops enter the country.

In March 1945, a Communist-led government is set up.

A People's Republic is proclaimed in December 1947. | Led by **Josip Broz Tito**, a war hero, the Yugoslav Communists form a government in March 1945.

In 1948, **Tito** refuses to acknowledge **Stalin**'s supremacy, and the Soviet Union breaks relations with Yugoslavia. From then on, **Tito** pursues an "independent road toward **socialism**." | **Cold War** starts during 1945-48.

In March 1946, Sir Winston Churchill coins the expression **Iron Curtain**.

In April 1949, **NATO** is established.

During 1948-49, the **U.S.** and other Allies supply blockaded West Berlin in the Berlin Airlift. | 1944-1950 |
			Diplomatic relations between the **U.S.S.R.** and Yugoslavia are restored.	The Korean War, during 1950-1953, claims 54,246 **U.S.** casualties.	1953
					1955
In October, Budapest rises in an anti-Communist revolt, but the uprising is brutally suppressed by the Soviet armed forces. **János Kádár**, with Soviet help, becomes the new leader of the country. Until 1989, the uprising would be officially labeled as **counterrevolution**.	In June, workers riot in Poznań, and Władysław Gomułka becomes the first secretary of the Communist Party; subsequently he introduces some liberal reforms and improves relations with the church.		Yugoslavia denounces the suppression of the Hungarian uprising.		1956
In June, Imre Nagy, prime minister during the 1956 uprising, is hanged for treason.					1958
				After one year in power, Fidel Castro has transformed Cuba into a strident Communist state.	1960

Fidel Castro's revolution transformed ▶ Cuba into the first Communist country in the Western Hemisphere.

1961

The U.S.S.R. installs nuclear missiles in Cuba, but under **U.S.** pressure the missiles are dismantled in October, in the Cuban Missile Crisis.

Albania breaks off relations with the Soviet Union, accusing **Khrushchev** of **revisionism**.

In August, the East German army erects the **Berlin Wall** and seals off West Berlin.

1963

In 1961, East Germany built the Berlin Wall ▶ around West Berlin. The wall stood for 28 years as a dramatic symbol of the Cold War.

1964

In October, **Khrushchev** is ousted and replaced by **Brezhnev**.

1965

The New Economic Model, giving individual enterprises more autonomy, is adopted.

1967

Following the Six-Day War, the U.S.S.R. condemns Israel and breaks off diplomatic relations.

The government closes all places of worship and declares the country an atheist state.

At a writers' congress in June, an open criticism of party leadership is voiced.

1968

In August, the U.S.S.R. leads a **Warsaw Pact** invasion of **Czechoslovakia** to crush the **Prague Spring**.

In September, the so-called **Brezhnev Doctrine** is formulated, justifying the right of the U.S.S.R. to intervene militarily in any Soviet-bloc country "in defense of **socialism**."

Albania formally withdraws from the **COMECON** and the **Warsaw Pact**.

In January, **Alexander Dubček** becomes the first secretary of the party and announces his goal of "**socialism** with a human face." The ensuing period of reform becomes known as the **Prague Spring**; it is crushed in August, when about 500,000 **Warsaw Pact** troops invade the country.

1969

In April, **Dubček** is replaced by Gustáv Husák.

1970

Czechoslovakia enters the period of "normalization," which freezes the country for two decades.

Willi Stoph, the chairman of the State Council, visits West Germany. It is the highest official visit since the founding of East Germany.

▲
The 1968 "Prague Spring" liberalization movement in Czechoslovakia flourished briefly before being crushed by Warsaw Pact troops.

18

HUNGARY	POLAND	ROMANIA	YUGOSLAVIA	THE WEST AND OTHER COUNTRIES	
Kádár puts forward the slogan, "Whoever is not against us is with us," in a first effort to heal the division of the country following the 1956 uprising.			The nonaligned movement of Third-World countries is formally inaugurated in Belgrade.	**U.S.** military involvement in Vietnam starts. In April, **U.S.**-trained Cuban exiles attempt to overthrow Castro's regime in the Bay of Pigs invasion.	1961
				In November, President John F. Kennedy is assassinated.	1963
In April, **Khrushchev** labels the Hungarian system "goulash **Communism**."			◄ *In 1963, President Kennedy signed a treaty that banned all but underground nuclear-weapon tests.*		1964
		In June, **Nicolae Ceauşescu** becomes the first secretary of the Communist Party.	Yugoslavia introduces far-reaching economic reforms, providing for workers' self-management.		1965
		Romania is the only Soviet-bloc country that does not break relations with Israel.		Israel is the winner in the Six-Day War with Arab states.	1967
The New Economic Mechanism is introduced in January, providing for economic decentralization.	In the spring, students in major cities riot, protesting censorship and political repression. The government subsequently embarks on an anti-Semitic campaign, and many Jews are forced to leave the country.	Romania supports the **Prague Spring** and denounces the August invasion of **Czechoslovakia** by **Warsaw Pact** forces.	Yugoslavia supports the **Prague Spring** and denounces the invasion of **Czechoslovakia** by **Warsaw Pact** forces.	In the spring, students riot in Paris against the Gaullist regime. In April, Martin Luther King, Jr., is assassinated; in June, Senator Robert Kennedy is shot and fatally wounded.	1968
				In July, the first **U.S.** astronauts land on the moon.	1969
	In December, a shipyard workers' protest is brutally suppressed, and at least 44 people are killed. Gomułka is replaced by Edward Gierek.			West German Chancellor **Willy Brandt** initiates his "Eastern policy" of improved relations with the Communist countries by visiting **East Germany**.	1970

19

1972

The U.S.S.R. and the **U.S.** conclude the SALT I treaty, limiting the number of offensive nuclear missiles.

East and West Germany conclude a treaty on economic, political, and cultural cooperation. The treaty also affirms the inviolability of their borders.

1973

Alexander Solzhenitsyn publishes his *Gulag Archipelago*, denouncing the Soviet penal system. Early the next year, he is expelled from the U.S.S.R.

▲
In 1972, U.S. President Nixon and Soviet leader Brezhnev signed the SALT I agreements, which limited the antiballistic missile systems of both countries.

1975

1977

Albania breaks off relations with China, accusing it of "social imperialist" policies.

In January, a human-rights manifesto called **Charter 77** is made public, and the authorities respond with a crackdown.

1978

A short-lived cultural "thaw" is initiated by **Zhivkov's** daughter, Lyudmila Zhivkova.

1979

In late December, the U.S.S.R. intervenes in Afghanistan.

The New Economic Mechanism, providing for decentralization of the economic policy-making in agriculture, is introduced.

1980

◄ *The U.S. Senate refused to ratify the SALT II agreements, signed by Soviet leader Brezhnev and U.S. President Carter in 1979, when the U.S.S.R. invaded Afghanistan.*

1981

Lyudmila Zhivkova dies, and the "thaw" initiated by her comes to an end.

West German Chancellor Helmut Schmidt visits East Germany.

In February, **U.S.** President Nixon visits China.

In May, President Nixon visits Moscow; it is the first visit to the **U.S.S.R.** by a **U.S.** president.

1972

In January, Vietnam peace pacts are signed in Paris.

In September, the Marxist government of Chile is overthrown.

1973

▲
Nicolae Ceaușescu ruled Romania for 25 years, beginning in 1964. His wife, Elena, was considered the second most powerful person in the country.

President Tito (below right, with an official visitor from China) made Yugoslavia into a relatively liberal socialist country.
▼

In August, 35 countries sign the **Helsinki Accords**, pledging inviolability of borders and respect for human rights.

1975

About 35,000 miners in the Jiu Valley strike because of economic grievances.

1977

Hungary establishes diplomatic relations with the Vatican.

In October, the archbishop of Cracow, Karol Cardinal Wojtyła, becomes Pope **John Paul II**.

1978

In June, **John Paul II** visits Poland.

The government introduces the New Economic-Financial Mechanism, providing for workers' self-management.

In January, the **U.S.** and China establish diplomatic relations.

1979

Workers begin to strike, and, in August, form an independent labor union, **Solidarity**. The strikers are led by **Lech Wałęsa**.

◀ *In 1981, Poland's Solidarity movement became the first independent trade union to be recognized in the Communist bloc.*

1980

In February, General **Wojciech Jaruzelski** becomes prime minister.

Dec. 13, **Jaruzelski** declares martial law, arrests the leadership of **Solidarity**, and suspends the union.

In January, **Ronald Reagan** becomes president of the **U.S.**

In March, Pope **John Paul II** barely escapes an assassination attempt.

1981

21

1982

Brezhnev dies in October and is succeeded by Yuri Andropov.

The New Economic Mechanism, providing for decentralization of the economic policy-making in industry, trade, and transport, is introduced.

1983

Italian investigators charge that Bulgarian agents were involved in the attempted assassination of Pope **John Paul II** in March 1981.

▲ *The Soviet invasion of Afghanistan turned into a 10-year guerrilla war against well-armed rebels.*

1984

Andropov dies in February and is replaced by Konstantin Chernenko.

Between December 1984 and March 1985, the government forces up to 1 million ethnic Turks (Muslims) to adopt Bulgarian and Christian names.

During 1984, 34,982 East German citizens are permitted to emigrate legally to West Germany.

1985

Chernenko dies on March 10 and, the same day, **Mikhail Gorbachev** becomes the new party secretary. He immediately begins his anticorruption and antialcoholism campaign.

In April, Enver Hoxha dies and is succeeded by **Ramiz Alia**.

The U.S.S.R. was widely ▶ *criticized for its secrecy following the nuclear accident at Chernobyl.*

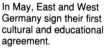

1986

In April, a nuclear accident happens at Chernobyl.

Gorbachev sets up two goals: **perestroika** (economic restructuring) and **glasnost** (political and social opening).

In March, the Italian court rules that there is insufficient evidence to prove Bulgarian complicity in the attempted assassination of Pope **John Paul II**.

In May, East and West Germany sign their first cultural and educational agreement.

Jan.-June 1987

On Jan. 28, the Communist Party Central Committee endorses **Gorbachev**'s proposals for economic and social reforms.

During the year, Albania establishes diplomatic relations with West Germany (in October), Jordan, Canada, Uruguay, and Bolivia.

On April 23, **Honecker** indicates that East Germany would not follow the Soviet model of **glasnost** and **perestroika**.

1982

In October, **Solidarity** is effectively dissolved.

In November, **Lech Wałęsa** is released after 11 months of internment.

▲ In 1983, a May Day demonstration by Solidarity supporters in Gdańsk, Poland, was violently dispersed by police.

1983

On July 22, martial law is lifted.

In October, **Lech Wałęsa** gets the Nobel Peace Prize.

1984

In July, the government announces a sweeping amnesty.

In October, a popular priest, Jerzy Popiełuszko, is murdered by two secret agents.

1985

In February, four security officers are convicted and sentenced to long prison terms for the murder of Father Popiełuszko.

In November, **Gorbachev** meets with President **Reagan** in Geneva.

1986

In September, the government announces a sweeping amnesty, which affects 71,500 people, including 1,070 political offenders.

▲ Father Popiełuszko, a popular priest murdered by Polish security police, quickly became a hero of the anti-Communist movement.

In December, Presidents **Gorbachev** and **Reagan** meet in Reykjavik, Iceland.

Jan.-June 1987

John Paul II visits Poland during June 8-14, and openly advocates political pluralism and human rights.

On May 25-27, **Gorbachev** visits Romania, but his speech on **glasnost** and **perestroika** is received without enthusiasm.

In early 1987, Yugoslav media report that there are about 500 political prisoners in the country, mostly ethnic Albanians.

In June, during his visit to West Berlin, President **Reagan** calls on **Mikhail Gorbachev** to tear down the **Berlin Wall**.

◄ The Catholic Church, led by John Paul II, the first Polish pope ever, helped inspire the Polish people to challenge Communist rule.

July-Dec. 1987

On Nov. 2, **Gorbachev** says that **Stalin** had committed enormous crimes.

On Nov. 11, the outspoken **Boris Yeltsin** is dismissed from the Moscow municipal party committee, after being accused by **Gorbachev** of excessive personal ambition and vanity.

In August, an article in the Writers' Union paper *Drita* accuses the Soviet Union of heading toward "barefaced capitalism."

Augustin Navrátil writes a 31-point petition calling for religious freedom. By September 1988, the petition gathers over 500,000 signatures.

On December 17, Gustáv Husák is replaced by Miloš Jakeš as party secretary, but retains his largely ceremonial post of president. In his speech, Jakeš verbally endorses **perestroika**.

During September 7-11, **Erich Honecker** visits West Germany; it is the first visit ever to West Germany by an East German head of state. **Honecker** pays a visit to his own birthplace in Neunkirchen, and also meets with his sister.

Jan.-Feb. 1988

On Feb. 8, **Gorbachev** announces that the pullout of Soviet troops from Afghanistan will begin on May 15, 1988, and will be completed within 10 months.

On Feb. 11, thousands of protesters in the **Nagorno-Karabakh** Region in **Azerbaijan** demand reunification with **Armenia**. On Feb. 28, at least 23 Armenians are killed in Sumgait.

Albania raises its diplomatic relations with **Bulgaria** to ambassadorial level.

On Feb. 23-26, Albania participates in the conference of foreign ministers of six Balkan countries in Belgrade. It is an important step out of Albania's diplomatic isolation.

On Jan. 28-29, the Bulgarian Communist Party holds a special party conference to discuss **perestroika**.

On Feb. 29, elections for municipal and regional councils take place; it is the first time that the ballot includes more than one candidate. Over a quarter of the elected deputies have been independent candidates, not affiliated with the Communist Party.

On Jan. 11, Miloš Jakeš visits Moscow for talks with **Gorbachev**. The latter says after the meeting that "innovative policies" are needed in Europe.

On Jan. 26-28, West German Chancellor **Helmut Kohl** visits Czechoslovakia; in addition to meeting with the officials, **Kohl** also meets with representatives of **Charter 77**.

On Jan. 7, **Erich Honecker** begins a three-day visit to France. President Mitterrand and Premier Chirac criticize East German human-rights practices and the existence of the **Berlin Wall**.

On Jan. 17, about 120 persons are arrested during a **dissident** demonstration in East Berlin.

March-April 1988

On March 13, *Sovietskaya Rossiya* newspaper publishes a letter by Mrs. Nina Andreyevna, attacking **glasnost** and **perestroika**. This conservative manifesto is said to be personally endorsed by **Ligachev**.

In March, several articles tentatively praise certain aspects of the Soviet **glasnost**. At the same time, however, the media criticize as "absurd" the current Soviet condemnations of **Stalin**.

On March 5-6, about 80 persons are arrested during human-rights manifestations in East Berlin and other cities.

May 1988

On May 7-9, a political opposition group known as the Democratic Union is founded in Moscow.

In 1988, many Soviet ▶ people turned out for celebrations marking the one-thousandth anniversary of the introduction of Christianity into Russia.

HUNGARY	POLAND	ROMANIA	YUGOSLAVIA	THE WEST AND OTHER COUNTRIES	
	On Nov. 29, in two related referenda, Polish voters do not endorse political and economic reforms proposed by the government. These are the first referenda ever to take place in a Communist country.	In November and December, antigovernment demonstrations take place in Braşov and several other places. The demonstrators protest against food shortages and restrictions on gas and electricity. On December 14, **Ceauşescu** says at the extraordinary party conference that Romania does not need any changes because it is on a path toward the "radiant summits of **communism**."	Tensions in the province of **Kosovo**, whose population is predominantly Albanian, increase, and, in October, emergency security measures are adopted.	A summit meeting between Presidents **Reagan** and **Gorbachev** takes place in Washington on December 7-10. The two leaders sign the Intermediate-Range Nuclear Forces Treaty and hail the meeting as a success.	July-Dec. 1987
	On Feb. 1, prices of goods and services rise an average of 27%, including 40% increases for basic food, 100% for gas and electricity, and 200% for coal. Protest demonstrations take place in Warsaw and Gdańsk.		On Feb. 24-26, Belgrade hosts a meeting of foreign ministers from **Albania**, **Bulgaria**, Greece, **Romania**, Turkey, and Yugoslavia. It is the first such regional meeting since the early 1930s.		Jan.-Feb. 1988
	On April 25, price increases spark a two-week wave of strikes, the gravest labor unrest since the imposition of martial law in December 1981.	On Apr. 5, the government announces that it intends to reduce the number of Romanian villages from about 13,000 to some 6,000 to 7,000, and replace them with "agro-industrial centers," in the so-called "systematization plan."	On March 14-18, **Gorbachev** visits Yugoslavia and admits that the rift between the **U.S.S.R.** and Yugoslavia dating from 1948 was the Soviet Union's fault.		March-April, 1988
On May 14, the first independent trade union (Trade Union of Scientific Workers) is formed. On May 22, **János Kádár** is replaced by Károly Grósz.				Between May 29 and June 2, President **Ronald Reagan** of the U.S. visits the **U.S.S.R.** It is Mr. **Reagan's** first visit to the country that he labeled "an evil empire" just a few years ago.	May 1988

June 1988

During June 5-16, celebrations of the 1,000th anniversary of the conversion to Christianity are held in the U.S.S.R.

On June 20, **Estonia** officially recognizes the People's Front of **Estonia**, which becomes the first non-Communist political group to gain official recognition in the U.S.S.R.

◀ *By means of a U.N.-mediated agreement, the U.S.S.R. began to withdraw its troops from Afghanistan in 1988. All the troops were home by mid-February 1989.*

Aug.-Sept. 1988

On Aug. 21, the 20th anniversary of the 1968 invasion, about 10,000 people demonstrate in the center of Prague. It is the largest public protest since 1969, but it is broken up by riot police and tear gas.

Oct. 1988

On Oct.1-2, the **Estonian** Popular Front for **Perestroika** holds its inaugural congress.

On Oct. 9, the **Latvian** Popular Front holds its founding congress.

On Oct. 10, Premier Lubomír Štrougal, the main advocate of economic reforms, is forced to resign.

On Oct. 10, about 80 persons are arrested in East Berlin during a demonstration against censorship of church publications.

Nov. 1988

On Nov. 22, eight people are killed and 126 wounded in violence between **Armenians** and **Azerbaijanis**.

Diplomatic relations with **Hungary** are raised to ambassadorial level.

On Nov. 3, 80 leading intellectuals found the Club for Support of **Glasnost** and **Perestroika.**

Dec. 1988

On Dec. 7, an earthquake registering 6.9 on the Richter scale strikes **Armenia**, killing at least 25,000 people.

◀ *In 1988, a strong earthquake in Armenia caused widespread destruction of property and untold suffering to the people.*

On Dec. 23, Bulgaria stops jamming Radio Free Europe.

On Dec. 1, **Honecker** criticizes the Soviet media for "attempting to rewrite Soviet history in a bourgeois manner."

HUNGARY	POLAND	ROMANIA	YUGOSLAVIA	THE WEST AND OTHER COUNTRIES	

Between 30,000 and 50,000 Hungarians demonstrate against the Romanian plan to raze as many as 7,000 ethnic Hungarian villages in **Romania** and replace them with agro-industrial complexes.

Local elections take place on June 19, but only 55% of voters participate, which is the lowest turnout since the beginning of Communist rule. **Solidarity** has called for the boycott of the elections.

▲
In October 1988, the Polish government announced plans to close the Lenin Shipyard in Gdańsk (above), the birthplace of Solidarity.

On Aug. 28, Hungarian Premier Grósz meets with the Romanian President **Ceauşescu** in an attempt to resolve disputes between Hungary and **Romania** concerning the Romanian plan to raze ethnic-Hungarian villages. The meeting is unsuccessful.

On Aug. 15, strikes begin in Silesian coal mines and quickly spread to other cities. The strikers demand the legalization of **Solidarity**. On Aug. 31, **Lech Wałęsa** begins discussions with the interior minister, Czesław Kiszczak, and then issues a call to the strikers to return to work.

On Sept. 19, former King Michael of Romania, exiled since 1947, issues a call in Switzerland for a revolt against **Ceauşescu**.

On Oct. 31, the government announces that it will shut down Gdańsk's Lenin Shipyard, birthplace and stronghold of **Solidarity**.

On Oct. 4-6, **Ceauşescu** visits the **U.S.S.R.** During the visit, **Gorbachev** indirectly criticizes Romanian policy and stresses the need for reform.

On Nov. 23, Miklós Németh replaces Communist Party Secretary Grósz as premier. Grósz remains general secretary.

Mrs. Thatcher visits Poland on Nov. 2-4 and urges the government to start a dialogue with **Solidarity**.

Jan. 1989

On Jan. 5, the Central Committee of the Communist Party calls for the mass rehabilitation of "thousands of victims" of the Stalinist purges from the 1930s to the early 1950s.

On Jan. 12, a special decree of the Presidium of the Supreme Soviet places **Nagorno-Karabakh** in **Azerbaijan** under direct rule from Moscow.

During Jan. 15-20, demonstrations take place in Prague, marking the 20th anniversary of the suicide of Jan Palach. The police break up the demonstrations with truncheons, water cannon, tear gas, and dogs. Among the persons arrested is the **dissident** playwright **Václav Havel**.

On Jan. 15, about 80 people are detained during a silent protest march in Leipzig.

Feb. 1989

By Feb. 15, all Soviet troops have left Afghanistan. In the nine-year war, about 15,000 Soviet troops were killed, and over 1 million Afghan combatants and civilians perished.

On Feb. 21, **Václav Havel** is sentenced to nine months in prison for "inciting anti-state and anti-social activities." Several other **dissidents** are tried on similar charges.

March 1989

In the March 26 elections for the Congress of People's Deputies, many Communist Party candidates are defeated by representatives of unofficial groups of independents. **Boris Yeltsin** wins a landslide victory in Moscow.

April 1989

On Apr. 9, a pro-independence demonstration in Tbilisi, **Georgia**, is brutally attacked by troops; 20 people die, either clubbed to death or killed by toxic gas.

On Apr. 20, **Andrei Sakharov** is elected to the Congress of People's Deputies.

◀ *Mikhail Gorbachev's policies of glasnost (openness) and perestroika (restructuring) have sent shock waves through Soviet society. One side effect of his programs has been the virtual elimination of the personality cult surrounding Lenin, whose statue or portrait once seemed to loom everywhere.*

HUNGARY	POLAND	ROMANIA	YUGOSLAVIA	THE WEST AND OTHER COUNTRIES	
On Jan. 11, a new law establishes the right to form new political parties. The official reevaluation of the 1956 uprising starts with the unauthorized statement by a leading reformer, Imre Pószgay, on Jan. 28, that the 1956 revolt was a "popular uprising," not a **counterrevolution**.	On Jan. 18, the plenum of the Central Committee of the Communist Party approves a resolution authorizing negotiations with **Solidarity** and its participation in roundtable discussions about Poland's future.		On Jan. 11, an opposition party calling itself the Democratic Alliance is inaugurated in Ljubljana, the capital of **Slovenia**. On Jan. 19, the collective state presidency designates **Ante Marković** the federal prime minister of Yugoslavia.	In January, **George Bush** becomes **U.S.** president.	Jan. 1989
On Feb. 16, the party historical commission publishes a report on the 1956 uprising, which rejects the designation **counterrevolution** and sharply condemns the Stalinist regimes imposed on the countries in **Eastern Europe**. On Feb. 22, the government announces that the anniversary of the 1917 October Revolution in **Russia** will no longer be celebrated in Hungary.	On Feb. 6, round-table talks between the authorities and the banned **Solidarity** union open. The first session, televised nationally, begins with addresses by the Interior Minister Czesław Kiszczak and by the **Solidarity** leader, **Lech Wałęsa**. In the second half of February, anti-Communist and right-wing opposition groups protest against the round-table talks.		On Feb. 2, a new opposition party called the Initiative for a Democratic Yugoslavia is formed in Zagreb, **Croatia**. Strikes by ethnic Albanians in **Kosovo** lead to resignation of the provincial party leadership; this provokes a Serbian backlash, which culminates in a 700,000-strong demonstration of Serbs in Belgrade against the "chauvinism and separatism" of Kosovar Albanians.	Western governments strongly protest against the sentences given to Czechoslovak **dissidents**, specifically to **Václav Havel**.	Feb. 1989
March 15 becomes the newly designated public holiday, commemorating the start of the 1848 Hungarian uprising against Austrian rule.		In early March, six former high officials accuse President **Ceauşescu** in an open letter of violating human rights and ruining the country's economy. The letter is published in the West on March 12-13.	On March 16, **Ante Marković** outlines his government program, which consists of a radical transformation of the Yugoslav economy to a free-market system. In early March, Serbian authorities ban public protests in **Kosovo**.		March 1989
On Apr. 22, the Communist Youth Union votes to dissolve itself. On Apr. 25, the **U.S.S.R.** begins a unilateral withdrawal of troops from **Eastern Europe**, starting with Hungary.	On Apr. 6, round-table talks between the authorities and the outlawed **Solidarity** conclude with the signing of three agreements: on trade union pluralism, political reforms, and economic and social policy. On Apr. 17, **Solidarity** is granted legal status.	On Apr. 12, 1989, the government announces that Romanian foreign debt had been paid back in full.		Student demonstrations in support of democracy start in China in mid-April.	April 1989

May 1989

On May 13-14, over 400 representatives of the **Estonian** and **Latvian** Popular Fronts and the **Lithuanian** Sajudis meet in Tallinn (Estonia) in the first Baltic Assembly.

On May 25, the Congress elects **Gorbachev** to the new post of chairman of the Supreme Soviet (that is, state president).

On May 31, **Boris Yeltsin** criticizes **Gorbachev** for the failures of **perestroika**, and also attacks the **nomenclature** (party and state bureaucracy).

On May 20-21, protests against "bulgarization" by ethnic Turks in northeastern Bulgaria turn violent. According to official accounts, seven people die, but the unofficial figure is 30.

On May 1, about 2,000 young people stage a pro-democracy demonstration, but are dispersed by the police.

On May 17, **Václav Havel** is released from prison after serving four months of his eight-month sentence. The authorities say that he is released because of "good behavior," but Western criticism is a more likely reason.

June 1989

On June 3-4, and again on June 7-8, a violent ethnic conflict takes place in **Uzbekistan** between Uzbeks and Meshketians. The toll is 99 dead and over 1,000 injured.

On June 16-17, ethnic violence takes place in **Kazakhstan**; the toll is four dead and 53 injured.

During June, over 80,000 ethnic Turks leave Bulgaria for Turkey.

On June 29, a petition called *A Few Sentences* is published. Signed by prominent **dissidents**, but also by many people from other sections of society, including the Communist Party, the petition sets out seven basic demands in order to "fundamentally change the social and political climate."

July 1989

On July 10, strikes begin in the Kuzbass coalfield in western Siberia. Within two weeks the strikes spread to the Donbass region of eastern **Ukraine** and to other mines.

On July 27-28, about 300 radical deputies (including **Boris Yeltsin** and **Andrei Sakharov**) form the "Inter-regional Group" within the Congress of People's Deputies, as an unofficial parliamentary opposition.

By the end of July, over 11,500 people sign *A Few Sentences.*

◄ *Andrei Sakharov, a leading Soviet physicist, emerged as an important dissident in the 1960s. In 1975, Sakharov won the Nobel Peace Prize for his human-rights activities. He spent six years in internal exile for his public opposition to Soviet policies before being released by Mikhail Gorbachev in 1986. In 1989, shortly before his death, Sakharov was elected to the U.S.S.R.'s Congress of People's Deputies.*

On May 2, Hungary begins to dismantle the barbed-wire fence on its border with Austria. This measure reportedly angers the authorities in **Czechoslovakia**, **East Germany**, and **Romania**.

On May 8, **János Kádár** is relieved of his post of party president and of his membership in the central committee.

▲ *Hungary's dismantling of the fence on its border with Austria sparked a huge exodus of refugees to the West.*

During May 15-18, **Gorbachev** visits China, and the state and party relations between China and the **U.S.S.R.** are formally normalized, after almost 30 years of tensions and animosity.

On May 17, over 1 million people participate in the largest antigovernment demonstration in Beijing, China.

May 1989

On June 13 and 21, the Communist Party leadership holds televised roundtable talks with representatives of political opposition groups.

On June 16, Imre Nagy, prime minister during the 1956 uprising, is reburied in a state funeral. The ceremony is attended by some 300,000 people.

On June 4 and 18, elections for the new bicameral National Assembly are held, and the **Solidarity**-backed candidates win all except one of the "unreserved" seats.

On June 6, **Jaruzelski** invites **Solidarity** to join the government in a broad coalition. **Solidarity** rejects this offer.

On June 3-4, Chinese troops crack down on pro-democracy demonstrations and kill an estimated 2,000 to 5,000 people.

On June 13, **Gorbachev** and **Kohl** sign a "historic" agreement on human rights and economic cooperation.

June 1989

On July 6, **János Kádár** dies. On the same day, the Hungarian Supreme Court repeals the treason verdicts that were handed down to Imre Nagy and eight of his associates during the 1956 uprising.

On July 11-12, President **Bush** visits Hungary, the first **U.S.** president to do so.

On July 9-10, President **Bush** visits Poland and meets with both **Jaruzelski** and **Wałęsa**. Poles are disappointed with the offered **U.S.** aid because they have expected a larger amount.

On July 19, **Jaruzelski** is elected to the new post of executive president of **Poland**.

On July 7-8, leaders of the **Warsaw Pact** states meet in Bucharest. Although the final communiqué unanimously endorses the current ideological diversity within the socialist bloc, it is reported that an "unprecedented disunity" reigned behind the scenes.

July 1989

31

THE SOVIET UNION	ALBANIA	BULGARIA	CZECHOSLOVAKIA	EAST GERMANY
Aug. 1989				
On Aug. 23, more than a million people in **Lithuania**, **Latvia**, and **Estonia** form a 360-mile-long human chain to commemorate the 50th anniversary of the Soviet-Nazi pact of 1939, which set the stage for the Soviet annexation of the **Baltic republics**.		By Aug. 21, the number of ethnic Turks fleeing from Bulgaria to Turkey has reached 310,000, and Turkey closes its borders.	On Aug. 21, on the anniversary of the 1968 **Warsaw Pact** invasion, several thousand demonstrators clash with the police, and almost 400 people are arrested.	
Sept. 1989				
On Sept. 8-10, the People's Movement of the **Ukraine** (referred to as Rukh) holds its founding congress. During September, the **Azerbaijan** Popular Front organizes a blockade of **Armenia**. On Sept. 19, at a meeting of the Central Committee, **Gorbachev** presents a program on nationalities policy, suggesting a restructuring of the Soviet federal system.			About 4,000 East Germans take refuge in the West German embassy in Prague during August and September.	Exodus of East Germans across the newly opened border between **Hungary** and Austria gains momentum, by the end of September, more than 24,000 East Germans have fled. New Forum, an umbrella organization set up to coordinate informal political groups, applies for official recognition, which is denied. Demonstrations start to take place regularly in Leipzig and other East German cities.
Oct. 1989				
On Oct. 9, a new labor law recognizes the right to strike; it is the first such recognition in Soviet history. Ethnic tensions continue in **Armenia**, **Azerbaijan**, and Ossetia in **Georgia**. On Oct. 13, **Gorbachev** strongly attacks certain editors and journalists for abusing **glasnost**. On Oct. 17, the published report by the Amnesty International notes that there has been a "dramatic" improvement in the Soviet human rights situation since 1986.	On Oct. 14, the Eco-Glasnost, an environmental group, begins collecting signatures on a pro-conservation petition. On Oct. 18, the Independent Association for the Defense of Human Rights stages its first rally, which is attended by about 160 people. On Oct. 23-24, the authorities start a clampdown on Eco-Glasnost and other unofficial groups, arresting more than 20 people.		On Oct. 28, up to 10,000 demonstrators protest in the center of Prague, and the police detain 355 persons. By the end of the month, the number of signatures on the petition *A Few Sentences* reaches 35,000.	On Oct. 1, a special train with about 4,000 East German refugees leaves Prague for West Germany. On Oct. 4-5, another train with 10,000 to 11,000 East Germans leaves Prague for West Germany. On Oct. 6-7, **Gorbachev** visits East Germany for the celebrations of its 40th anniversary. He reportedly warns **Honecker** that leaders who stay behind "put themselves in danger." On Oct. 18, **Erich Honecker** resigns for "health reasons" and is replaced by Egon Krenz. On Oct. 30, the weekly protest in Leipzig is attended by more than 300,000 people.

During August, a series of negotiations between the Communists and **Solidarity** culminates in a complete realignment of Polish politics when, on Aug. 24, the parliament elects as prime minister **Tadeusz Mazowiecki**, a leading **Solidarity** member. It is the formal end of the Communist era in Poland.

◀ *In August 1989, Tadeusz Mazowiecki (center) was elected prime minister of Poland, the first non-Communist to achieve that position in any Warsaw Pact country.*

Aug. 1989

Roundtable talks between the authorities and opposition groups end in a compromise agreement on Sept. 18. The agreement provides for free elections in 1990.

About 600 East Germans take refuge in the West German embassy in Warsaw during August and September.

On Sept. 12, **Mazowiecki** forms a new coalition government dominated by **Solidarity** members.

On Sept. 27, the parliament in **Slovenia** proclaims the republic an "independent, sovereign, and autonomous state," with a right to secession from the Yugoslav federation.

During Sept. 9-18, **Boris Yeltsin** visits the **U.S.**, on a private lecture tour.

Sept. 1989

Huge demonstrations became a ▶ *regular feature of Czechoslovakia's "velvet revolution" in late 1989.*

During Oct. 6-10, the Hungarian Socialist Workers' Party (the Communist Party) is fundamentally restructured and renamed the Hungarian Socialist Party. The new party pledges its commitment to multiparty democracy and market economy.

On Oct. 17-20, the parliament approves an amended constitution, describing Hungary as an "independent democratic state."

On Oct. 23, the anniversary of the 1956 uprising, the name of the country is formally changed to the "Republic of Hungary."

On Oct. 10, Poland's first stock exchange opens in Warsaw.

On Oct. 12, the government publishes a plan for a quick establishment of a full-fledged market economy.

On Oct. 26-27, foreign ministers of the **Warsaw Pact** countries meet in Warsaw and reject the so-called **Brezhnev Doctrine**. They announce a new policy of recognizing the absolute right of each state to determine its development, which is being referred to popularly as the **Sinatra Doctrine** (the **Warsaw Pact** countries can "do it their way").

Oct. 1989

33

Nov. 1989

On Nov. 4-7, the **Armenian** National Movement holds its founding congress.

On Nov. 17-19, the Supreme Soviet of **Georgia** reaffirms the republic's right to secede from the Soviet Union.

On Nov. 27, the **U.S.S.R.** Supreme Soviet grants the **Baltic republics** full right over their resources and autonomy in financial operations.

On Nov. 28, the Supreme Soviet returns the rule over **Nagorno-Karabakh** to **Azerbaijan**.

On Nov. 15, Albania declares an amnesty, which applies to a limited number of political prisoners.

On Nov. 3, about 4,000 people take part in a pro-democracy demonstration outside the National Assembly. It is the largest unofficial demonstration in Bulgaria since 1947.

On Nov. 10, **Todor Zhivkov** is ousted in a "palace coup" and replaced by Petur Mladenov, the foreign minister. Mladenov promises free elections and stresses the urgency of "turning Bulgaria into a modern democratic and law-governed state."

On Nov. 17, an official rally of over 100,000 supports political reforms.

On Nov. 17, an officially approved student demonstration turns into a violent clash with the police.

On Nov. 20, a "demonstration week" begins, with protest rallies growing in numbers and spreading throughout the country.

On Nov. 27, a two-hour general strike is supported by millions of workers.

On Nov. 29, the article guaranteeing the "leading role of the Communist party" is abolished.

On Nov. 4, over 500,000 demonstrate in East Berlin.

On Nov. 7, the whole Politburo of the Communist Party resigns.

On Nov. 8, the New Forum opposition group is legalized.

On Nov. 9, the **Berlin Wall** is opened and several million East Germans visit West Berlin in the first few days.

On Nov. 17, the new prime minister, Hans Modrow, says that speculation about German reunification is "as unrealistic as it is dangerous."

Dec. 1989

On Dec. 1, **Mikhail Gorbachev** meets with **John Paul II**. It is the first meeting ever between a pope and a Soviet head of state.

On Dec. 7, the **Lithuanian** Supreme Court deletes the article guaranteeing the "leading role" of the Communist Party.

On Dec. 14, **Andrei Sakharov** dies of a heart attack.

On Dec. 19-20, the Communist Party of **Lithuania** declares itself independent of the Communist Party of the Soviet Union.

On Dec. 11, **Zhivkov** is expelled from the Communist Party.

On Dec. 10, a new federal government is formed in which the non-Communists have a majority. The same day, President Husák resigns.

On Dec. 17, the border with Austria is opened.

On Dec. 20, the extraordinary congress of the Communist Party adopts a statement apologizing to the Czechoslovak people for "unjustified reprisals" after 1968.

On Dec. 28, **Alexander Dubček** is elected chairman of the Federal Assembly.

On Dec. 29, **Václav Havel** is elected president of the republic.

On Dec. 1, the parliament abolishes the leading role of the Communist Party.

On Dec. 3, a human chain of up to 2 million people joins hands across East Germany, calling for democratic renewal.

On Dec. 7, round-table talks are held with the opposition, and the participants agree that general elections will be held in May 1990.

On Dec. 16-17, the Communist Party changes its name from the "Socialist Unity Party" to "Socialist Unity Party—Party of Democratic Socialism."

◀ *Millions of East Germans visited West Berlin in the first few days after the Berlin Wall was opened.*

On Nov. 26, a referendum narrowly approves the petition of opposition groups to postpone the election of a president after the legislative elections in March 1990.

On Nov. 20-24, the 14th congress of the Romanian Communist Party is held, and **Ceauşescu** is elected for a further five-year term as the general secretary.

On Nov. 28, West German Chancellor **Helmut Kohl** presents a plan for a German confederation that could eventually lead to reunification.

◄ *Romania's overthrow of the Ceauşescu dictatorship was by far the most violent of the 1989 revolutions in Eastern Europe.*

On Dec. 29, the parliament approves a radical economic-reform package, to begin on Jan. 1, 1990.

On Dec. 29-30, the formal name of the country is changed to "Polish Republic" (instead of Polish People's Republic).

On Dec. 16, several hundred people protest a deportation order served on a Protestant pastor, Fr. Lázsló Tökes, in Timişoara. Next day, the protests grow larger, and the police fire on the crowd.

On Dec. 22, **Ceauşescu** and his wife are airlifted from the Central Committee headquarters as demonstrators break into the building. The revolutionaries organize themselves into the National Salvation Front (NSF).

On Dec. 25, **Nicolae** and Elena **Ceauşescu** are tried before a military tribunal; condemned to death; and immediately executed.

By Dec. 25, **Ion Iliescu** is named president by the NSF.

On Dec. 28, the country's name is changed to Romania (rather than the Socialist Republic of Romania).

By December, relations between **Slovenia** and **Serbia** deteriorate considerably, leading to the effective closure of the border between the two republics.

On Dec. 2-3, Presidents **Bush** and **Gorbachev** meet aboard **U.S.** and Soviet warships off the coast of Malta for their first summit.

▲ *U.S. President Bush and Soviet President Gorbachev developed a friendly rapport during their first summit meeting in Malta.*

THE SOVIET UNION	ALBANIA	BULGARIA	CZECHOSLOVAKIA	EAST GERMANY
Jan. 1990 On Jan. 11, the Supreme Soviet of **Latvia** abolishes the "leading role" of the Communist Party. On Jan. 11-13, **Mikhail Gorbachev** visits **Lithuania**, on a mission to solve the secessionist crisis. On Jan. 19, Soviet troops assault the city of Baku, **Azerbaijan**, following the escalation of ethnic violence between **Armenians** and **Azerbaijani** that has erupted early in January.	On Jan. 1, **Ramiz Alia** says in his New Year's message that the country's enemies are renewing "a campaign of slanders" against Albania. He further states that Albania is a "society of justice" without "social conflicts or national oppression." According to second-hand testimony, anti-Stalinist demonstrations take place on Jan. 11 and 14 in the city of Shkodër, involving up to 7,000 people.	On Jan. 1-2, anti-Turkish demonstrations break out in southern Bulgaria. On Jan. 15, the parliament repeals the article guaranteeing the "leading role" of the Communist Party. On Feb. 2, the 14th extraordinary congress of the Communist Party states in its manifesto that the party is now committed to "human and democratic **socialism**."	On Jan. 2, President **Havel** visits **East** and West **Germany**. On Jan. 25-26, President **Havel** visits **Poland** and **Hungary**.	Throughout January, roundtable talks with opposition groups continue. On Jan. 15, thousands of protesters ransack the headquarters of the secret police in Berlin. On Jan. 28, Prime Minister Hans Modrow announces the formation of a government of national responsibility, which includes eight opposition ministers.
Feb. 1990 On Feb. 5-7, the Central Committee backs **Gorbachev**'s new platform that clears the way for a multiparty system in the U.S.S.R. On Feb. 23, the Supreme Soviet of **Estonia** abolishes the article guaranteeing the "leading role" of the Communist Party.		On Feb. 8, after the opposition groups refuse to join a new coalition government, the National Assembly approves a government that consists solely of Communist ministers. On Feb. 25, the opposition alliance called Union of Democratic Forces organizes a rally at which 200,000 participate.	On Feb. 1, the secret police is abolished. During Feb. 17-22, President **Havel** visits Iceland, Canada, and the **U.S.** On Feb. 26-27, **Havel** visits Moscow and confers with **Gorbachev**. They sign an agreement that all 73,500 Soviet troops stationed in Czechoslovakia will depart by July 1991.	On Feb. 1, upon his return from the **U.S.S.R**, Prime Minister Hans Modrow proposes to create a united, neutral Germany. On Feb. 5, the government of national responsibility is installed, with a majority of non-Communists. On Feb. 13-14, Hans Modrow visits West Germany.
March 1990 On March 11, the Supreme Soviet of **Lithuania** declares the republic independent. On March 13, the Congress of People's Deputies abolishes the monopoly of the Communist Party. On March 14, **Mikhail Gorbachev** is elected President of the U.S.S.R. On March 30, the Supreme Soviet of **Estonia** agrees to set in motion a process of secession from the U.S.S.R.		On March 5, the National Assembly adopts a bill that allows ethnic Turks to resume their original names that they had been compelled to renounce during the forced assimilation in 1984-85. On March 6, the National Assembly legalizes strikes for the first time in Bulgarian history.	Throughout March, the Federal Assembly is engaged in a "hyphen war"—a prolonged debate about the new name of the country. The Slovaks, inhabitants of **Slovakia** in the eastern part of the country, want the name to be spelled "Czecho-Slovakia," but the Czechs reject this spelling.	On March 18, the first free and secret general elections are held in East Germany. The winning party, the Christian Democratic Union, gets 40.8% of the vote; the Communists get 16.4%.

On Jan. 5, the "Danube-gate" scandal breaks open when it is revealed that the Interior Ministry security police have not stopped covert surveillance of opposition politicians, despite amendments creating a multiparty system.

On Jan. 27, the Polish Communist Party (named Polish United Workers' Party) decides to disband itself at its 11th and final congress. The gathering then becomes a founding congress of a new party, the Social Democracy of the Polish Republic.

On Jan. 3, the NSF reverses the former regime's prohibition of foreign borrowing.

On Jan. 12, the NSF outlaws the Communist Party of Romania, but the next day the decision is reversed.

On Jan. 28-29, large demonstrations take place in Bucharest, first by the opponents of the National Salvation Front, and then by supporters.

On Jan. 2, Yugoslavia introduces a new dinar worth 10,000 old dinars, in an effort to bring down inflation, which has reached 1,125% in December.

On Jan. 20-23, the 14th extraordinary congress of the Communist Party (League of Communists of Yugoslavia) takes place, but it ends in disarray after the delegation from **Slovenia** walks out.

At the end of January, violence erupts again in the province of **Kosovo**.

Jan. 1990

By 1990, Lithuanians (above) and other residents of the Baltic Republics had become very vocal in their demand for independence from the Soviet Union.

On Feb. 1, the National Salvation Front agrees to share power with representatives of 29 opposition parties.

On Feb. 18, about 3,000 to 8,000 demonstrators demand **Ion Iliescu**'s resignation. Next day, 5,000 to 8,000 miners from the Jiu Valley are brought to Budapest in support of the National Salvation Front.

On Feb. 4, the League of Communists of **Slovenia** renounces its links with the League of Communists of Yugoslavia.

On Feb. 13, the four major World War II Allies—France, the **U.S.S.R.**, England, and the **U.S.**—and the two German states agree on a "two-plus-four" formula for the unification of Germany.

On Feb. 25, the opposition candidate wins the presidency in Nicaragua against the candidate of the Sandinistas.

Feb. 1990

On March 10, an agreement is signed with the **U.S.S.R.** providing for the complete withdrawal of all 52,000 Soviet troops from Hungary by July 1991.

On March 25, the first round of general elections takes place.

On March 1, the Timișoara Declaration calls for the banning of ex-Communists from public offices.

On March 20, about 2,000 Romanian nationalists attack a peaceful demonstration by 5,000 ethnic Hungarians in Transylvania.

March 1990

37

THE SOVIET UNION	ALBANIA	BULGARIA	CZECHOSLOVAKIA	EAST GERMANY

April 1990

On Apr. 6-7, an extraordinary congress of the **Latvian** Communist Party takes place, and ends in a split into independent and pro-Moscow parties.

On Apr. 18, the U.S.S.R. begins an economic blockade of **Lithuania**.

On Apr. 17, **Ramiz Alia** says at the Central Committee's plenum that Albania is no longer opposed to diplomatic ties with the **U.S.S.R.** and with the **U.S.**

On Apr. 3, Petur Mladenov is elected president of Bulgaria.

On Apr. 3, the Communist Party renames itself the Bulgarian Socialist Party.

On Apr. 9, a meeting of Czechoslovak, Hungarian, and Polish leaders is held in Bratislava, to discuss the "return to Europe" of the three countries.

On Apr. 20, the Federal Assembly adopts the new name of the country: Czech and Slovak Federative Republic.

On Apr. 12, a new "grand coalition" government led by the Christian Democratic Union is sworn in.

May 1990

On May 1, following the May Day parade, about 40,000 people from opposition groups denounce Communist rule and President **Gorbachev**.

On May 4, the Supreme Soviet in **Latvia** proclaims **Latvia's** independence from the U.S.S.R.

On May 8, the Supreme Soviet in **Estonia** proclaims **Estonia** independent.

On May 29, **Boris Yeltsin** is elected president of **Russia**.

On May 7-8, the People's Assembly approves judicial and economic reforms and lifts the ban on religious propaganda. According to unofficial reports, there have been demonstrations in several Albanian towns in the previous months.

◄ *At Moscow's 1990 May Day Parade, thousands of demonstrators denounced the Communist government.*

On May 18, a treaty on "the creation of a monetary, economic, and social union" between the two Germanys is signed.

June 1990

On June 12, **Russia** is declared a sovereign state.

On June 20, the Supreme Soviet of **Uzbekistan** declares the republic sovereign.

On June 23, the Supreme Soviet of **Moldavia** adopts a declaration of sovereignty.

On June 29, **Lithuania** suspends its declaration of independence, and Moscow lifts its economic blockade.

On June 10 and 17, free elections are held. The Communist Party, renamed Socialist, receives 47% of the vote.

On June 8-9, the first free elections since 1946 are held. The victors are the Civic Forum in the Czech lands, and its counterpart in Slovakia, Public Against Violence, with 47% of the vote. Communists receive almost 14% of the vote.

On Apr. 8, the second round of general elections takes place, and the center-right Hungarian Democratic Forum wins 41.6% of the votes.

On Apr. 13, the Soviet authorities admit Soviet responsibility for the Katyn Forest massacre.

On Apr. 19-20, **Solidarity** holds its first major national conference since 1981.

On Apr. 7-8, the NSF meets in its first national conference and calls for a democratic multiparty system.

On Apr. 11, the National Salvation Front bars former King Michael of Romania from entering the country.

On Apr. 8, a center-right coalition called DEMOS wins in the first free elections in **Slovenia**.

On Apr. 22, the first round of elections in **Croatia** takes place.

On May 16, Prime Minister Jozsef Antall forms a coalition government.

On May 27, the first fully free elections take place, for local councils. **Solidarity**-backed candidates win 41% of the seats, but only 42% of voters participate in the elections.

On May 20, in the first free elections in Romania since 1937, the National Salvation Front wins 66.3% of the votes, and **Ion Iliescu** wins the presidency with 86% of the votes.

On May 6-7, the second round of general elections takes place in **Croatia**, and the winning party is the right-wing nationalist Croatian Democratic Union.

On May 5, the first round of "two-plus-four" talks on the reunification of Germany takes place in Bonn.

On May 29, representatives of 40 countries sign the founding charter of the European Bank for Reconstruction and Development, which is intended to finance the economic rehabilitation of **Eastern Europe**.

During June 13-15, violent confrontation takes place in Bucharest between anti-Communist demonstrators and pro-government miners brought into the city. The toll is six people dead and about 500 injured.

Between May 31 and June 3, Presidents **Bush** and **Gorbachev** hold their second summit in Washington.

◄ *In December 1989, dissident playwright Václav Havel was elected president of Czechoslovakia. He received a visit from Pope John Paul II in April 1990.*

	THE SOVIET UNION	ALBANIA	BULGARIA	CZECHOSLOVAKIA	EAST GERMANY
July 1990	On July 10, at the 28th party congress, **Gorbachev** is reelected general secretary. On July 11, **Yeltsin** quits the Communist Party.	In early July, about 5,000 Albanians seek refuge in foreign embassies and are eventually allowed to leave the country. On July 31, Albania and the **U.S.S.R.** restore diplomatic relations.	On July 6, Mladenov is forced to quit because of charges that he wanted to use tanks against demonstrations in December 1989.	On July 6, **Václav Havel** is reelected president for a two-year term.	On July 1, East and West Germany become united economically with one currency. On July 16, seven nations (England, France, the **U.S.**, the U.S.S.R., **East Germany**, West Germany, and **Poland**) agree on unification of the two Germanies.
Aug. 1990			On Aug. 1, Zhelyu Zhelev, leader of the Union of the Democratic Forces, is elected president.		
Sept. 1990	On Sept. 13, a new German-Soviet friendship pact is signed, allowing the united Germany to play a major role in the changing Soviet economy.				
Oct. 1990	On Oct. 1, the U.S.S.R. Supreme Soviet passes a law guaranteeing full religious freedoms. On Oct. 2, **Lithuania** and the U.S.S.R. agree to conduct their economic relations as equal partners. On Oct. 17, the Ukrainian parliament bows to student demands and agrees to support the Ukrainian independence.			On Oct. 11, thousands rally in Prague in an anti-Communist demonstration. On Oct. 17, Finance Minister Václav Klaus is elected chairman of the Civic Forum. He is the most outspoken advocate of free-market economy.	At the stroke of midnight on Oct. 2, East Germany ceases to exist as it voluntarily merges with West Germany. About 1 million people celebrate at the Brandenburg Gate in Berlin.

◀ *In July 1990, thousands of Albanians who had sought refuge in foreign embassies were allowed to leave the country aboard ships sailing under the United Nations flag.*

	THE SOVIET UNION	ALBANIA	BULGARIA	CZECHOSLOVAKIA	EAST GERMANY
Nov. 1990	On Nov. 17, **Gorbachev** presents a new emergency power structure, in which he would rule together with the Federation Council representing the 15 republics. After several days, the plan is rejected by **Yeltsin** as insufficient.		Throughout the month, antigovernment rallies take place in Sofia. The government is forced to resign on Nov. 29.	On Nov. 24, local elections take place; Communists win 17% of the vote.	
Dec. 1990	Germany begins airlifting emergency food supplies to the U.S.S.R.	On Dec. 9, a large student demonstration takes place in Tirana.		**Havel** asks for special powers to prevent the breakup of Czechoslovakia.	

On July 5, **Serbia** suspends the parliament of **Kosovo**.

◄ *On October 2, 1990, amid much celebration, Germany became a united country for the first time since the end of World War II.*

On Aug. 3, the writer Arpád Göncz, member of the Alliance of Free Democrats, is elected Hungarian president.

During Aug. 21-27, antigovernment demonstrations take place in Bucharest.

On Aug. 2, Iraq invades Kuwait.

On Sept. 17, **Wałęsa** declares his presidential cadidacy against **Mazowiecki**.

On Sept. 12, a treaty between WWII Allies and the two Germanys ends the Allied powers' responsibility over Germany.

On Oct. 15, the ruling party, Hungarian Democratic Forum, is beaten in local elections. Less than 30% of eligible voters participate.

On Oct. 26, taxi and truck drivers block traffic throughout the country, protesting gas price hikes.

On Oct. 18, the government presents a radical plan for a transition to a market economy.

On December 9, 1990, Lech Wałęsa won the presidency of Poland in a landslide election.
▼

On Nov. 25, **Mazowiecki** resigns after losing the first round of presidential elections.

On Nov. 19, 35 nations, members of the **Conference on Security and Cooperation in Europe** sign a treaty limiting conventional weapons systems in Europe.

On Dec. 9, **Wałęsa** is elected president of Poland in a landslide victory.

On Dec. 2, **Kohl** is elected chancellor of the united Germany.

July 1990

Aug. 1990

Sept. 1990

Oct. 1990

Nov. 1990

Dec. 1990

41

UPHEAVAL IN EUROPE:
An Alphabetical Overview

Albania. Probably the poorest country in Europe, Albania has always been on the outskirts of European history. Bordering on **Yugoslavia**, Greece, and the Adriatic Sea, Albania is about the size of Alabama, and the population is just over 3 million.

Despite centuries of foreign rule, Albanians have preserved a separate identity. They gained their independence in 1920, but during World War II were annexed by Italy. Communist guerrillas fought the Italian and German forces, and, in 1944, a Communist government led by Enver Hoxha was established.

Between 1946 and 1990, Albania was a harshly ruled Stalinist country, with a pervasive **personality cult** surrounding the party chief Hoxha until his death in 1985. Professing a fierce self-reliance, Albania broke with the **U.S.S.R.** for its **revisionism** and with China for its "social impe-

In late 1990, bleak Albania was the only Eastern European country still committed to Stalinism.

rialism" (whatever that means), prohibited any borrowing from the West, and, by the end of the 1970s, stood virtually alone in the world.

Albania is shockingly poor: in the countryside, you see almost no machinery, individual citizens are forbidden to own automobiles, and cities at night are quiet and dark, with streetlamps no stronger than pocket flashlights. The basic needs are assured, however, and because the poverty is so uniformly spread and most Albanians are profoundly ignorant about life in other countries, one could encounter—at least until recently—a certain sense of national achievement and progress and a pride of independence.

Until 1990, Albania considered itself the only state truly following the precepts of **Marxism-Leninism**—the government even prohibited religion and, in 1967, closed down all places of worship. The winds of **glasnost** and **perestroika** finally penetrated into the country, and, by the summer of 1990, there were clear signs that even in Albania, times were out of joint.

Demonstrations—something unheard of for the past 46 years—occurred in Tirana and other places in January, spurred on by the events elsewhere in **Eastern Europe**, by economic grievances, and by the lessening of fear of the security forces, known as *Sigurimi*. In the spring of 1990, President **Ramiz Alia** announced a program of "democratization," allowing farmers to cultivate private plots, making foreign travel more accessible, and permitting Albanians to practice religious rites in the privacy of their homes.

However welcome this move was, it did not calm the restive population. In July, in the most serious postwar political upheaval, about 5,000 Albanians stormed foreign embassies and were then allowed to leave the country; many others allegedly crossed the borders without papers, risking their lives, into **Yugoslavia** and Greece.

Ramiz Alia then ousted several hard-liners from the Politburo, and also issued decrees allowing foreign investment (which had been banned since 1967) and giving the Albanians a limited right to gather in public demonstrations. But the times of political calm are gone, and the population is fidgety. It is only a question of time before this last European bastion of Stalinism crumbles down.

Alia, Ramiz (1925-), first secretary of the Albanian Communist party (formally known as the Albanian Workers' Party) since 1985, Alia does not command anything like the reverence lavished on his predecessor, Enver Hoxha, but many Albanians speak of him with respect. Although he was a longtime Hoxha colleague, Alia now wants to be considered a reformist. He seems to understand the need for change, but is very cautious and does not want to let the reform process get out of hand. Foreigners describe him as a man of charm and self-confidence, but even though he has been promoting a certain degree of "democratization" (while talking at the same time about "our socialist ideal"), the question is whether he would be able to move swiftly enough to stay abreast of history, or whether he would be swept away as so many other Communist leaders have been during the past few years.

Antisocialist. The word has been used since the times of **Stalin**, but became especially popular in the 1970s and 1980s, when it was hurled with great gusto at all actual and potential dissidents, and at anyone who might even think of disagreeing with the party line, especially in the **U.S.S.R.**, **Czechoslovakia**, **East Germany**, **Romania**, and **Bulgaria**.

Armenia, a Soviet republic in the Caucasus region, slightly larger than Maryland and with 3.4 million people, has an almost 2,000-year-old history. In the 4th century, Armenia accepted Christianity, and, in the 5th century, a monk called Mastoc created a special alphabet that is still in use today. After alternating periods of independence and foreign rule (by Turkey and Persia), Armenia became part of the Russian Empire in the early 19th century.

Until **Gorbachev** came to power, Armenia was slumbering in the gray uniformity of Soviet life. Since the late 1980s, however, it has become a protagonist in the most severe ethnic conflicts in the **U.S.S.R.**, over a region called **Nagorno-Karabakh**, which lies within **Azerbaijan**

Ethnic conflicts have plagued Azerbaijan and Armenia during the past several years.

but is inhabited mostly by Armenians. The hostility toward the Azerbaijani has deep historical roots and involves economic, religious, and ethnic differences.

In August 1990, the Armenian parliament changed the name of Armenia from "Soviet Socialist Republic of Armenia" to "Republic of Armenia" and declared its independence from the **U.S.S.R.**

Azerbaijan is a Soviet republic in the Caucasus, somewhat smaller than Indiana and a little larger than South Carolina, inhabited by a predominantly Muslim population of 6.7 million. Since 1988, Azerbaijan has been in a bitter conflict with **Armenia** over a small region within its territory called **Nagorno-Karabakh**, which has historical significance for both Armenians and Azerbaijani. The conflict feeds on deep historical roots and on religious, ethnic, and economic differences between the Christian, Indo-European, and generally more affluent Armenians, and the Muslim, Turkic, and economically worse-off Azerbaijani. In September 1989, **Azerbaijan** adopted a declaration of sovereignty.

In January 1990, at least 60 people were killed in an anti-Armenian pogrom in Baku, the Azerbaijani capital. Fighting erupted in several other places, and, on January 19, Soviet troops mounted an assault on Baku. The official death toll was 83 dead, but unofficial sources put the number of people killed as high as 600. At the funeral of the victims of the assault, 750,000 people filled the streets of Baku, and thousands of Azerbaijani party members burned their party membership cards.

Baltic Republics, three Soviet republics—**Lithuania**, **Latvia**, and **Estonia**—that were forcibly integrated into the **U.S.S.R.** in 1940-41, on the basis of the secret protocols appended to the Soviet-Nazi pact of 1939. In May 1990, the presidents of the republics reestablished the Baltic Council, which had existed between 1934 and 1940, in order to coordinate their efforts to gain independence.

Belorussia is the third-largest republic of the **U.S.S.R.**, on the Soviet border with **Poland**; it is a little smaller than Kansas and has a population of 10 million. The Belorussians are ethnically very close to the Russians (or Great Russians), and there has been a lot of intermingling, which accounts for the fact that Belorussia has not seen any strong nationalist stirrings, in contrast to other Soviet republics. Nevertheless, a sovereignty resolution was passed by the Supreme Soviet in July 1990.

Berlin Wall. At the end of World War II, Berlin was partitioned into four sectors, three under the Western Allies and one under the **U.S.S.R.** After the creation of the Federal Republic of Germany and the German Democratic Republic in 1949, Berlin remained divided, but since the crossing points between East and West Berlin could not fully control all the traffic, Berlin represented a major crack in the **Iron Curtain**. On August 13, 1961, the borders between East and West Berlin were closed and, in the following days, a 5-foot-tall concrete wall was erected, topped with broken glass and barbed wire.

When thousands of East Germans began to flood the West German embassies in Prague and in Warsaw, the beleaguered East German leadership headed by Egon Krenz decided on November 9, 1989, to open

For over 28 years, the Berlin Wall divided Communist East Berlin from capitalist West Berlin.

the borders. Within a few days, millions of East Germans crossed into West Berlin. A joke at that time told of **Erich Honecker** waking up at night and finding all East Berlin brightly illuminated but empty; whereupon he goes to the Wall and finds a note stuck in a crack, with a message, "The last one to leave please put out the lights."

Brandt, Willy (1913-), was the chancellor of the Federal Republic of Germany during 1969-74, and, in 1971, received the Nobel Peace Prize for his policy of opening to the East (the so-called *Ostpolitik*). When Brandt arrived on his first visit to **East Germany** in May 1970, he was welcomed with an overwhelming enthusiasm wherever he appeared. He was the chief architect of the so-called Basic Treaties that the two Germanies signed in 1972.

Brezhnev, Leonid (1906-85), first secretary of the Communist Party of the **U.S.S.R.** from 1964 until his death in 1985. Growing up under **Stalin**, he ascended to power after the ouster of **Khrushchev** in 1964. An authoritarian leader but not a supreme dictator, Brezhnev apparently ruled with the consensus of his colleagues in the party Politburo. He was a conservative hard-liner and, especially in his later years, a man who wanted to maintain the status quo at all costs; later, the years of his rule were labeled the "period of stagnation."

During the early 1970s, which saw the beginnings of **détente**, Brezhnev visited the **U.S.** several times and met with Presidents Nixon and Ford; he also signed the SALT I accord in 1972, limiting antimissile systems and certain offensive weapons. In his final years, he was a pitiful sight: he could barely walk and speak, yet he clung to power until his last breath.

Brezhnev (left, with West German leader Helmut Schmidt) ruled the Soviet Union for 21 years.

Brezhnev Doctrine was unofficially formulated in the fall of 1968, after the invasion of **Czechoslovakia** by **Warsaw Pact** troops. The doctrine implies that the **U.S.S.R.** can use its armed forces in order to "defend **socialism**" in an allied Communist country.

Bulgaria is a hilly Balkan country that borders the Black Sea in the east, **Romania** in the north, **Yugoslavia** in the west, and Greece and Turkey in the south; it is the size of Tennessee, and the population is about 9 million. The capital, Sofia, was founded by the Romans in the 2nd century. Although the Bulgarians speak a Slavic language, they are the descendants of a mixture of Slavic tribes and central Asian Turkic tribes of Bulgars, who invaded the Balkan Peninsula in the 7th century. The early Bulgarian state adopted Christianity in the 9th century, then came under foreign rule, rose again in the 12th and 13th centuries, but soon after that was conquered by Ottoman Turks. In 1878, Bulgaria became independent thanks to Russian pressure on the Ottomans, and from this time dates the Bulgarians' deeply felt friendship with the Russians.

When Bulgaria became Communist in 1944, the violence against political opponents was exceptionally widespread, but as the country gradually settled in its Communist ways and the initial reign of terror subsided, the Bulgarians—because of their historical affinity with the Russians—generally felt less alienated from their regime than did the central European Communist countries. The Bulgarian party leadership remained unquestionably loyal to Moscow, and there were almost no known dissidents or protests comparable to those in **Hungary**, **Poland**, or **Czechoslovakia**.

During the 1980s, Bulgaria twice became an object of international attention—first when a connection of Bulgarian agents with the unsuc-

Despite decades of official atheism, many Bulgarians remain devoted members of the Orthodox Church.

cessful assassination of Pope **John Paul II** was being investigated in 1982 and 1983, and then in the middle of the decade, when the Bulgarian government embarked on a forcible "Bulgarization" campaign, decreeing that all ethnic Turks were in fact Bulgar Slavs, and that they must take Bulgar and Christian names, instead of their Turkish and Muslim ones. The campaign was accompanied by violence, and several people died. In the late spring of 1989, another forcible "Bulgarization" drive led to violence and death and a mass exodus of more than 300,000 ethnic Turks from Bulgaria to Turkey.

In October 1989, a few dissident groups held their first rallies while an international conference on environment took place in Sofia. The presence of foreign delegations compelled the government to show a certain tolerance. On November 3, about 4,000 people demonstrated in front of the National Assembly; it was the largest unofficial demonstration since 1947. On November 10, the second-longest-ruling Eastern European leader, **Todor Zhivkov**, was forced to resign in a palace coup, and was replaced by his former foreign minister, Petur Mladenov. Subsequently, hard-liners were dismissed from the Politburo, and several reformists were reinstated.

In January 1990, the government initiated talks with opposition groups, united in an umbrella organization called the Union of Democratic Forces. Its leader, Dr. Zhelyu Zhelev, was one of a handful of Bulgaria's dissidents. The Bulgarian opposition, however, was still too immature to present any real challenge to the Communists, who renamed themselves Socialists and, in free elections in June, won 48 percent of the vote.

Shortly after the elections, hundreds of anti-Communist students built up tents in a "Communist-free zone" in Sofia, and finally succeeded in forcing the resignation of Mladenov based on accusations that he had wanted to use force against demonstrators in December 1989. In August, the Bulgarian parliament chose Zhelyu Zhelev to become president—the first non-Communist president since World War II.

Bulgaria continues to be the only Eastern European country where the old Communist machinery survived with very few changes. Nonetheless, the opposition is growing stronger. At the close of 1990, the shortages of virtually everything—gasoline, bread, cheese, milk, cooking oil, shoes, socks, baby clothes, and aspirin—have driven people into the streets in huge antigovernment demonstrations that ultimately forced the government to resign in late November 1990.

Bush, George (1924-), the forty-first president of the **United States**, has presided over the end of the **Cold War**. In the first year and a half of his presidency, he treated the changes in the **U.S.S.R.** and in **Eastern Europe** with extreme caution, but in June 1990, when **Gorbachev** visited the **U.S.**, President Bush spoke of a "new era" and, in November 1990, at the meeting of the **Conference on Security and Cooperation in Europe**, he declared that the **Cold War** was over.

Ceauşescu, Nicolae (1918-89). General secretary of the Romanian Communist Party from 1965, Ceauşescu began as a Romanian nationalist who won admiration both in **Eastern Europe** and in the West for his defiance of the **U.S.S.R.** in matters of foreign policy. He condemned the invasion of **Czechoslovakia** in 1968, and, in the early 1970s, became a frequent visitor in Western capitals; twice he came to the **U.S.**, in 1970 and 1973.

Ceauşescu also concentrated on building his own power and on creating a family dynasty. His wife, Elena, despite less than a high-school education, became the head of the National Council for Science and Technology, and was increasingly praised as one of the world's leading scientists; his brothers and children were all also placed in high positions.

In 1982, Ceauşescu's decision to pay off all foreign debt plunged **Romania** into both virtual and metaphorical darkness (only very low-

*Construction of Ceauşescu's grandiose Palace of the People
ceased immediately upon the dictator's downfall.*

watt bulbs were permitted). At the same time, he began to build in downtown Bucharest a mammoth white-marble-covered Palace of the People, which has hundreds of offices and thousands of rooms, and such extravaganzas as a 980-bulb chandelier. While the Romanian people had barely enough to eat, and froze in their insufficiently heated apartments, Ceauşescu devoted time every Saturday to pester architects at the building site of the oversized structure. The Romanian government now wonders what to do with this unfinished building: make it into a casino, a museum of the atrocities of Stalinism, a university, or a Dracula park?

The dramatic demise of Ceausescu was seen by millions of television viewers around the world: his utter disbelief when he was heckled during an official rally on December 20, his defiance at the hastily arranged trial several days later, and finally his crumpled body minutes after the execution on December 25. He never seemed to grasp what was happening.

Charter 77 was the name of a manifesto issued by a group of 242 dissidents in early January 1977: among its first signatories was the future president of **Czechoslovakia, Václav Havel**. The manifesto, worded in cautious language, listed some basic human-rights demands. It provoked a furious backlash from the authorities, who thus in fact popularized the text. Many signatories, whose number grew to over 1,000, were arrested, forced into exile, or otherwise harassed, but the group of dissidents formed at that time remained the nucleus of the dissident movement for the next 12 years.

Cold War. During World War II, the **U.S.S.R.** was one of the four major Allies who fought against Germany, but the alliance did not survive for long. Signs of tensions between the **U.S.S.R.** and the West appeared as

The evacuation of Soviet troops from Czechoslovakia was a sure sign that Cold War tensions had eased.

early as late 1945; in the following years, the tensions developed into a full-blown rupture, and the world soon divided into two hostile camps. During the following four decades, the Cold War was most clearly expressed in regional conflicts—whenever something happened in the world, the **U.S.** and the **U.S.S.R.** were always on opposite sides. The Cold War was at its most intense in the early 1950s. The following three decades were still characterized by antagonism, but there were also periods of more-friendly relations, particularly the **détente** during the 1970s. After the **U.S.S.R.** invaded Afghanistan in December 1979, the relations between the superpowers turned hostile again.

By 1990, the Cold War had been officially proclaimed dead. The first test of the new world order has been the crisis in the Middle East, after Iraq invaded Kuwait in August 1990: it was the first time since World War II that the **U.S.S.R.** and the **U.S.** stood on the same side during a regional conflict.

COMECON, or **CMEA** (standing for Council for Mutual Economic Assistance), an economic grouping of Communist countries, was founded in 1949, and, by 1990, comprised **Bulgaria**, **Czechoslovakia**, **East Germany**, **Hungary**, **Poland**, **Romania**, and the **U.S.S.R.**, and Cuba, Mongolia, and Vietnam outside of Europe (**Albania** was a member from 1949 to 1968). The organization was intended to promote the "socialist economic organization," but was never really an efficient body, and its only achievement was its supervision of sufficient supplies of cheap oil and raw materials from the **U.S.S.R.** to **Eastern Europe**.

Communism is a word dating from the mid-19th century. The vision of Communism as a classless, economically just society was first formulated by Karl Marx in his *Communist Manifesto* of 1848. The first sentence

Communist countries celebrate May Day, the official labor holiday, with parades and demonstrations.

of the booklet read, "The specter of Communism is stalking Europe," and it proved to be correct, albeit in a different way than Marx had in mind. The manifesto concluded with a ringing appeal, "Workers of the world, unite!", and the phrase later became one of the magic formulas of the Communist world. In a bitter joke, one banner at the unofficial rally during the 72nd anniversary celebration of the **October Revolution** in Moscow in 1989 carried a paraphrase, "Workers of the world, forgive us."

Conference on Security and Cooperation in Europe grew out of the **Helsinki Accords**, signed by 35 countries in 1975. The crowning achievement of the conference is the treaty limiting conventional weapons systems in Europe, concluded in Paris on November 19, 1990.

Counterrevolutionary was a very strong and dangerous word—stronger than **antisocialist**, to label the opponents and critics of the Communist regimes.

Croatia is one of the six constituent republics of **Yugoslavia**, twice as large as Maryland, with 4.6 million people. Croatia had its first free elections in the spring of 1990; the winner was a nationalist right-of-center party, the Croatian Democratic Union. Croatia, together with **Slovenia**, wants to change the present federal system of **Yugoslavia** into a much looser confederacy. The main problem for the republic, however, is the Serbian enclaves, which account for 11 percent of Croatia's population.

Czechoslovakia is a country in the center of Europe of about the same size as the state of New York, but in an elongated shape stretching west-east between Germany and the Soviet Union. Its population of some 15 million includes 63 percent Czechs, 31 percent Slovaks, 4 percent Hungarians, and a small number of Germans and Poles.

Czechoslovakia is a 20th-century creation: rising on the ashes of the Austro-Hungarian Empire at the end of World War I, it has combined the historic lands of Bohemia and Moravia with **Slovakia**, inhabited by Slovaks, close linguistic cousins of Czechs and Moravians. Until 1938, Czechoslovakia was a well-functioning progressive liberal democracy, but it disintegrated under the onslaught of Nazism.

Communist rule became established in February 1948, in a bloodless coup, and in the following massive purges and show trials, the new leaders eliminated all real and potential opposition. When **Khrushchev** initiated his policy of **de-Stalinization**, there were no reformist rulers in Czechoslovakia, and so the Stalinist regime persisted into the early 1960s. Then, jolted by a sudden economic crisis, the leadership embarked on economic reforms and also began to introduce political liberalization. This gradual reformist process culminated in the **Prague Spring** of 1968, led by the reformist Communists headed by **Alexander Dubček**. This eight-month period was crushed by a **Warsaw Pact** invasion in August 1968.

The new hard-line leadership, under Gustáv Husák, purged the party of everyone even remotely suspected of reformist inclinations (over 500,000 party members were either expelled or resigned) and "bribed" the general population by significantly raising living standards. The country plunged into a stuporous period of "normalization," during which most people retreated into a private "exile" of purely personal concerns. Only a handful of brave men and women, loosely grouped around the **Charter 77** movement, continued to oppose the official repression.

In the late 1980s, Czechoslovak leaders started to pay lip service to the "new thinking" coming from the **U.S.S.R.**, but it was just empty words, and the population at large was profoundly skeptical about the possibility of political liberalization. Almost imperceptibly, however, the society was changing: more and more people were willing to speak out; more and more young people challenged the police.

The country first stirred from its slumber on August 21, 1988, the 20th anniversary of the invasion by the **Warsaw Pact** in 1968: about 20,000 demonstrators surprised the police and everyone else. It took 15 more months and a number of other demonstrations, petitions (especially

Czechoslovakians have eagerly embraced the freedoms won in 1989's "velvet revolution."

a brief manifesto penned in the summer of 1989 and called *A Few Sentences*), and other acts of defiance to finally culminate in the "velvet revolution" of November-December 1989.

In the summer and early fall of 1989, citizens of Czechoslovakia wistfully followed the rapid pace of events elsewhere in **Eastern Europe**— the first non-Communist prime minister in **Poland**, the disintegration of Communist power in **Hungary**, the exodus of East Germans, the breaching of the **Berlin Wall**, and the fall of **Zhivkov** of **Bulgaria**—and still skeptically expected that political changes in Czechoslovakia were far off. But the brutal beating of students on November 17 was the straw that broke the camel's back, and within a few weeks, the top of the Communist pyramid, no longer supported by Soviet tanks, fell off. On December 10, the country had its first predominantly non-Communist government since 1948. Later in the month, the still predominantly Communist parliament elected a brilliant intellectual, **Václav Havel**, as president.

Czechoslovakia entered 1990 still full of euphoria and surprise at how smooth and easy it all was. In the first free elections, in June 1990, Civic Forum and its Slovak counterpart, Public Against Violence, easily won over other parties. By the end of 1990, the exhilaration at the newly won freedoms had been replaced by the everyday reality of problems looming ahead: how to eliminate the surviving **nomenclature** in high economic posts, how to dismantle the complex system of command economy, how to solve the nationalist tensions with **Slovakia**, and how to learn democratic ways.

De-Stalinization was initiated by **Nikita Khrushchev** shortly after his "secret speech" in February 1956 in which he denounced **Stalin**'s reign of terror. For millions of people both in the **U.S.S.R.** and abroad, **Stalin** had been a supreme hero, and so **Khrushchev**'s revelations came as a tremendous shock. The "secret speech" soon became known in the West, but in the **U.S.S.R.**, it was not published until early 1989.

    Khrushchev's de-Stalinization consisted mostly of the following:
- The vast prison system, or gulag—as later described by **Solzhenitsyn**—was largely dismantled, and thousands of prisoners were released.
- A cultural "thaw" (or liberalization) was introduced, which permitted the publishing of unorthodox authors.
- The **personality cult** was gradually eliminated.
- Dialogue with the West was initiated, and **Khrushchev** became the first Soviet leader to visit the **U.S.**

Détente, which means relaxing or easing of political tensions between countries, started in 1970 when **Willy Brandt** embarked on his policy of conciliation with **East Germany**. Then, in 1972, President Richard Nixon visited China and the **U.S.S.R.**, and **Brezhnev** had several summit meetings with **U.S.** and West European leaders. The détente culminated in the **Helsinki Accords** of 1975 and ended with the Soviet invasion of Afghanistan in December 1979.

Dissident. As a term designating a dissenting individual or group in Communist countries, the word came into a general use in the 1970s. Dissidents were harassed, accused of **antisocialist** acts, sometimes put in prison, and then increasingly exiled to the West, the most famous case being the forced exile of **Aleksandr Solzhenitsyn** in early 1974. All the dissident movements, with the exception of Polish **Solidarity**, were numerically small, but they represented the seeds of the forthcoming revolutionary upheaval. Former dissidents are now presidents, prime ministers, and high officials in the new Eastern European and Soviet governments.

Dubček, Alexander (1921-), known in the West as the leader of the **Prague Spring**, was born a few months after his parents had returned from Chicago to their native **Slovakia**, and then spent his youth in the **U.S.S.R.** When he was elevated to the Czechoslovak Communist Party leadership in January 1968, Dubček was an unknown apparatchik. But when he announced his program of "**socialism** with a human face," he turned into a symbol of the euphoric eight-month liberalization period. After August 1968, Dubček was gradually demoted, then expelled from the party and made a "nonperson." In the late 1980s, he began to reemerge, and in the first days of the "velvet revolution" in November 1989, he came to Prague. In late December, he was elevated to the chairmanship of the Federal Assembly.

Eastern Europe. This term has been used to designate the European Communist countries, but since Europe extends from the Atlantic in the west to the Ural Mountains in the east, "Eastern Europe" is geographically not correct: **Poland**, **Czechoslovakia**, **Hungary**, and the former **East Germany** lie in the center of Europe. The people in these countries have always felt part of Western European civilization.

The southern four countries belonging to the political group of "Eastern Europe"—**Romania**, **Bulgaria**, **Yugoslavia**, and **Albania**—are more properly the Balkan countries, which historically have been that part of southern Europe influenced by Orthodox Christianity and the Ottoman Empire.

East Germany was a Communist German state known formally as the German Democratic Republic, which lasted from October 7, 1949, until October 2, 1990, that is, 40 years and 360 days. Almost the same size as Tennessee, with 16 million people, East Germany bordered on **Poland** in the east, **Czechoslovakia** in the southeast, West Germany in the south and west, and the Baltic Sea in the north.

In 1945, defeated Nazi Germany was divided into four occupation zones, and as the World War II Allies—the **U.S.**, Britain, France, and the **U.S.S.R.**—drifted apart in the first years of the **Cold War**, the three western zones became the Federal Republic of Germany in 1949, and shortly after that, the eastern zone administered by the **U.S.S.R.** was constituted into the German Democratic Republic.

The first half of East German existence, closely linked with the tenure of the hard-liner Walter Ulbricht, was characterized by a stringent hostility toward West Germany, which culminated in the erection of the **Berlin Wall** in 1961. The second half, under the leadership of **Erich Honecker**, was ushered in by **Willy Brandt**'s "Ostpolitik," a policy of conciliation between the two German states.

East Germany took years to recover from the devastation of World War II.

East Germans visiting West Berlin were spellbound by the quantity of consumer goods available there.

In 1953, shortly after its birth, East Germany was shaken by a wave of strikes. These were quickly suppressed, and during the following decades, there was no significant **dissident** activity in the country. In the 1980s, an unofficial peace movement developed within the Protestant churches and became a haven for those opposed to the regime. The activists were harassed, and many were forced to emigrate.

Economically better off than people in other Communist states, East Germans had two major grievances: they were constantly comparing themselves to their wealthier West German kin, and they bitterly resented the impossibility of foreign travel. It was not really surprising that when the **Iron Curtain** along the Austro-Hungarian border cracked in the summer of 1989, East Germans started pouring through. Their dramatic exodus, initially across **Hungary** and later through West German embassies in Prague and Warsaw, was followed by millions of television viewers throughout the world. Then came the demonstrations, first of thousands, but soon tens of thousands and ultimately hundreds of thousands of people, many who chanted, "We want to stay," and demanded changes. The southern city of Leipzig began to hold weekly marches each Monday evening, and there were demonstrations in other major cities.

Erich Honecker resigned on October 18 and was replaced, both as party leader and as head of state, by Egon Krenz, who had his moment of glory on November 9, when he ordered the **Berlin Wall** opened. Soon, however, Krenz was swept away into the whirlpool of history.

New Forum, a dissident umbrella group formed in September, was officially recognized in early November. Later in the month, the former reformist mayor of Dresden, Hans Modrow, became the prime minister. Although Modrow first rejected the speculations about German reunification as "unrealistic" and "dangerous," he could not stop the tide, and, in fact, became one of those who helped pave the way to one Germany. But he, too, was pushed aside when, in the first free East German elections, in March 1990, the Christian Democratic Union (a newly formed sister party of the West German Christian Democrats) captured 41 percent of the vote. The leader of the victorious party, Lothar de Maizière, then assumed the premiership.

Meanwhile, West German Chancellor **Helmut Kohl** was energetically pursuing his plan for reunification in countless meetings with East German leaders, Western heads of state, and of course **Mikhail Gorbachev**—because the **U.S.S.R.** still continued to have troops in East Germany. In March, the "two-plus-four" (two Germanies plus the **U.S.**, Britain, France, and the **U.S.S.R.**) talks on reunification opened in Bonn. The most important hurdle was overcome in July, when Gorbachev agreed to the membership of the united Germany in **NATO**. On September 12, the *Final Settlement with Respect to Germany* was signed by the victorious World War II Allies and by the two Germanies. It was the formal end of World War II.

This treaty opened the way to German reunification, which took effect at midnight on October 2, 1990. East Germany ceased to exist, and was incorporated—as five newly constituted states—into the Federal Republic of Germany.

Estonia, the northernmost of the three **Baltic Republics**, is about twice the size of Massachusetts. Estonians, who number only 1.5 million, are related to Finns. In February 1990, the Estonian Supreme Soviet abolished the "leading role of the party," and, the following March, the government declared its intention to start negotiations about secession from the **U.S.S.R.**

Georgia is a Soviet republic in the Caucasus, somewhat larger than West Virginia and smaller than South Carolina. Its 5 million inhabitants, proud heirs of a more than 2,000-year-old history, are known for their entrepreneurial spirit. The most famous (or rather infamous) Georgian was Iosif Vissarionovich Dzhugashvili, who early in his career adopted the pseudonym **Stalin**.

In April 1989, in one of the worst cases of brutality in the **U.S.S.R.** in recent years, Soviet troops attacked a nationalist demonstration in the capital, and clubbed 20 people to death. The troops also used toxic gas. Ethnic conflicts with Abkhas, inhabitants of a region within Georgia, continued throughout the year. In November 1989, Georgia declared its sovereignty.

Glasnost has become a household word throughout most of the world. It means "openness," and it refers mostly to the open public debate about social, political, and economic matters, and, very important, about the country's past. Glasnost is one of the means to achieve **perestroika**, a complete transformation of the Soviet system.

In some ways, glasnost has been a traumatic experience for many Soviet citizens, especially the older ones, because after more than seven decades, every tenet of the official belief system has been questioned and attacked, and nothing seems certain anymore.

Mikhail Gorbachev's policies of glasnost and perestroika have transformed the Communist world.

Gorbachev, Mikhail (1931-), general secretary of the Communist Party of the **U.S.S.R.** since March 1985, president of the **U.S.S.R.** since March 1990, and a Nobel Peace Prize winner in 1990. Well educated and a forceful personality, Gorbachev differs from all the previous Soviet rulers in several important aspects: he does not share their distrust or fear of the West, he is no dogmatic, he is willing to learn from his mistakes, and, despite his enormous personal power, he is no dictator—he has let himself time and time again be publicly subjected to harsh questions, heckling, and attacks, and he has always taken it in stride.

His ambitious revolutionary goal of transforming the Soviet system and society, through **glasnost** and **perestroika**, is still very much in the future, and many doubt whether it is attainable at all. Like the man who let the genie out of the bottle, Gorbachev set loose so many forces and long-suppressed emotions that he can no longer control them. In the fall of 1990, his popularity at home plummeted to an all-time low, while that of his main rival, **Boris Yeltsin**, went up. But the verdict on Gorbachev must still wait.

Gorbachev has been clearly successful in foreign policy. His influence and "blessing" was a crucial factor in the fall of Communist regimes in **Eastern Europe** and in the reunification of Germany. He counts as friends many Western leaders, and bears the greatest credit for the end of the **Cold War.**

Havel, Václav (1937-), playwright, writer, and president of **Czechoslovakia**. Born into a wealthy family, Havel was not admitted to a secondary school because he was branded a "class enemy." One of the founders of the **Charter 77** movement, he spent over four years in prison, the last time in the spring of 1989. In November of that year,

Much of Vaclav Hável's presidency has centered on controlling Czechoslovakia's secessionist movements.

Havel led the Czechoslovak "velvet revolution" as head of Civic Forum, and, in December, was elected president of the country.

Helsinki Accords were the first document of the **Conference on Security and Cooperation in Europe**, signed in 1975 in Helsinki. The document guaranteed the inviolability of European borders and included pledges to respect human rights. In late 1970, **dissident** "Helsinki groups" emerged in many Communist countries and demanded from their governments a respect for human rights.

A 1980 demonstration in London protested Soviet violations of the Helsinki Accords.

Honecker, Erich (1912-), was the leader of the East German Communist Party (known formally as the German Socialist Unity Party) from 1971, and head of **East Germany** as chairman of the State Council until he was deposed in October 1989. He presided over a conciliation between the two Germanies and, in 1987, became the first East German head of state to visit West Germany. When **Mikhail Gorbachev** shook the Communist world with his **glasnost** and **perestroika**, however, Honecker did not like it, claiming that the East German economy and society did not need any reforms. He soon found himself fatally out of step with history.

Hungary is a flat, landlocked country in the center of Europe, somewhat smaller than Indiana. It has a population of 10 million. Hungarians are descendants of warrior nomad Magyar tribes, which came to central Europe from Asia in the 9th century. Gradually, they settled down, accepted Christianity, and formed an important medieval kingdom.

In the 19th century, Hungary gained internal autonomy within the Austro-Hungarian Empire. When the empire collapsed at the end of World War I, Hungary lost about two-thirds of its territory—to the newly formed **Czechoslovakia**, to **Romania**, and to **Yugoslavia**. Significant Hungarian minorities continue to live in those countries, the largest being in Romanian Transylvania.

In 1941, Hungary joined World War II on the side of Germany. After the war, the Hungarian Communists took power with the help of the Soviet occupying forces. An anti-Communist and anti-Soviet resentment persisted, however, and finally, in 1956, grew into an open revolt. The armed uprising of October, which had been preceded by political ferment and liberalization, seemed at first to be succeeding, and Hungary proclaimed neutrality and withdrew from the **Warsaw Pact**. But in early November, the uprising was brutally suppressed by Soviet forces: the estimates of people killed range from 6,500 to 32,000. About 250 participants, including the hero of the uprising, Imre Nagy, were later executed.

Then began the era of **János Kádár**, who was installed as premier by the Soviets. Universally hated at that time, he later began to implement political and economic reforms and gained much respect for his policies. The Hungarian system, branded by **Nikita Khrushchev** as "goulash **Communism**," gradually evolved into one of the most liberal Communist regimes.

In the late 1980s, the authority of the Hungarian Communist Party began to erode, and despite efforts by reformist Communists and the removal of **Kádár** to a ceremonial post in May 1988, the party was on an irreversible slide to disintegration. In June 1989, Imre Nagy was reburied in a state funeral, and the party leadership initiated roundtable talks with the main opposition groups. Around that time, an official reevaluation of the 1956 uprising took place, and it was no longer called a **counterrevolution**. In October, the Hungarian Communist Party (formally known as the Hungarian Socialist Workers' Party) was formally dissolved and reconstituted as the Hungarian Socialist Party. At the same time, opposition groups crystallized into several distinct groupings, the major ones being the Hungarian Democratic Forum (appealing to nationalist Hungarian sentiments) and the Alliance of Free Democrats (representing urban intellectuals and former dissidents).

Even under Communist rule, Hungarian grocery stores usually had an abundant supply of fresh foods.

Meanwhile, Hungary opened its borders with Austria in the summer of 1989, and thousands of East Germans vacationing in Hungary decided to head west. This movement grew like an avalanche and, within a few months, mushroomed into the final fatal crisis of hard-line Eastern European Communist regimes.

Hungarians might have felt a little cheated because their transition to the post-Communist era has been relatively quiet and undramatic. The first free elections since 1946 took place in March and April 1990, and the Forum emerged as winner. The reformed Communists received only 11 percent of the vote.

During 1990, Hungary concentrated on its economic reform, primarily the privatization of state enterprises. As the year drew to a close, another economic complication arose: the price of gasoline. At the end of October, the government raised fuel prices by 60 percent. Taxi and truck drivers became so enraged that they blockaded major roads and some border crossings. The government then lowered the prices somewhat, but a sense of trauma persisted, as well as a growing fear of all the side effects of the economic transition ahead.

Iliescu, Ion (1930-), leader of the Romanian National Salvation Front, was elected president of **Romania** in May 1990, with 85 percent of the vote. Iliescu had studied in Moscow, and then held senior posts in regional administration, but in the 1980s was pushed aside by **Ceauşescu**. During 1990, the antigovernment opponents charged that Iliescu was a reform Communist whose commitment to democracy and market economy was not sincere.

Iron Curtain. In a speech in Missouri on March 15, 1946, Sir Winston Churchill said that "an Iron Curtain has descended over the continent." Inadvertently, Churchill had coined the precise term that for decades would describe the heavily fortified and virtually impenetrable border between the West and the Communist countries. The Iron Curtain stretched from the Baltic Sea in the north to Trieste, **Yugoslavia**, in the south. A new part was added in 1961, with the erection of the **Berlin Wall**.

Jaruzelski, Wojciech (1923-), general of the Polish army, he became prime minister in March 1981, during the heyday of **Solidarity**. Under intense Soviet pressure to do something about the **antisocialist** forces in the country, he declared martial law in December 1981 and had the Solidarity leaders and activists arrested, including **Lech Wałęsa**.

In July 1989, Jaruzelski was elected president, a position he retained until the presidential elections in November 1990.

John Paul II (1920-). Karol Wojtyła, archbishop of Cracow from 1963, was elevated to the papacy in 1978, the first Slavic pope ever to occupy the highest office in the Roman Catholic Church. He greatly contributed to the determination of his Polish compatriots to challenge **Communism**.

In December 1989, John Paul II had a 75-minute private audience with **Mikhail Gorbachev**, the first meeting ever between a pope and a Soviet leader. When **Stalin**, dismissing the church as totally irrelevant, sarcastically asked, "How many divisions does the pope have?", he would have been appalled if he could have envisioned this meeting.

Kádár, János (1912-89), Hungarian Communist leader between 1956 and 1988. Coming to power during the 1956 uprising, with Soviet backing, Kádár became known as the "butcher of Budapest." In 1961, however, he put forward the slogan, "Whoever is not against us is with us," and thus initiated a period of normalization. A sweeping amnesty in 1962 and subsequent economic liberalizations made **Hungary** the most liberal country in **Eastern Europe**.

In the late 1980s, however, Kádár became increasingly rigid and resistant to reforms. In May 1988, was "kicked upstairs" to the largely ceremonial post of party president.

As Polish prime minister, Jaruzelski (center, at a wreath-laying ceremony) led the crackdown on Solidarity.

Kazakhstan is a Central Asian Soviet republic, four times the size of Texas and with a population of 16 million. By the early fall of 1990, Kazakhstan and **Kirghizia** were the only Soviet republics that had not proclaimed their sovereignty.

Khrushchev, Nikita (1894-1971), Soviet leader who began his political career under **Stalin**. After the dictator's death, he shocked the Soviet Communist Party and the rest of the world with his "Secret Speech" of February 1956, in which he denounced **Stalin**'s crimes and initiated the period of **de-Stalinization**. Khrushchev was a timid precursor of **Gorbachev**, but times were not yet ripe for reform, and he was forced out of office in 1964. In the last years of his life, he secretly dictated his memoirs, which appeared in the West. The last installment, called the *Glasnost Tapes*, was published in the fall of 1990.

Kirghizia is a Central Asian Soviet republic, about as large as South Dakota and with 4 million people. Rioting in June 1990 between Kirghiz and Uzbeks resulted in almost 200 people dead and over 1,000 injured.

Kohl, Helmut (1930-) West German chancellor and architect of German reunification. He pursued this goal with great perseverance, partly because he was aware of the mixed feelings of West Germans about reunification: they would have to bail out the decrepit East German economy. One of Kohl's greatest moments was in July 1990, when he emerged from a long meeting with **Gorbachev** and announced that the last hurdle had been overcome, and the **U.S.S.R.** had agreed to the participation of the united Germany in **NATO**. In December 1990, Kohl was elected chancellor of the unified Germany.

Kosovo is a small region in southern **Serbia**, one of the six republics of **Yugoslavia**. Most people living in Kosovo are ethnic Albanians, and, since late 1988, there has been an escalating conflict between the local

The Kosovo region of Yugoslavia has been racked by conflict between ethnic Albanians and native Serbians.

Albanians and the Serbian authorities. In 1974, Kosovo was made an autonomous province within **Serbia**, but this status was canceled in the summer of 1990 when the Serbian authorities took direct control. Increasingly, people in Kosovo talk about an armed uprising and secession from **Yugoslavia**.

Latvia, one of the three **Baltic Republics**, lies between **Estonia** in the north and **Lithuania** in the south. It is almost the same size as West Virginia and has just 2.6 million inhabitants, out of whom only 53 percent are ethnic Latvians, but like its neighbors, wants to be independent from the **U.S.S.R.** In May 1990, its Supreme Soviet passed a resolution declaring Latvia's independence.

Ligachev, Yegor (1920-). The most vocal opponent of **perestroika**, Ligachev has battled the tide of changes in the **U.S.S.R.** with great resolve but with little success. In July 1990, at the 28th party congress, Ligachev angrily proclaimed that "thoughtless radicalism, improvisation, and swinging from side to side have yielded us little good during the past five years of **perestroika**." Although he received enthusiastic applause, he was soundly defeated by a "perestroichik" candidate in an election for the second highest party post, the deputy general secretary.

Lithuania is the southernmost of the three **Baltic Republics**, slightly larger than West Virginia and with a population of 3.6 million. The last nation in Europe to accept Christianity, in the 14th century, the medieval Lithuania embraced a much larger territory than the present republic, and often was at loggerheads with **Russia**.

In March 1990, Lithuania declared its independence, and, in mid-April, the **U.S.S.R.** introduced an economic blockade. Despite efforts to gain international recognition, no Western government accepted the Lithuanian declaration, but rather, urged both Moscow and Lithuania to behave with restraint. The conflict seemed finally solved in June, when

In 1990, President Landsbergis (right) and Premier Prunskiene (center) emerged as leaders of Lithuania's independence movement.

Lithuania suspended its declaration, and Moscow ceased its blockade. Then, in January 1991, Soviet troops moved in to suppress the independence movement, killing numerous civilians.

Marković, Ante (1924-), a **Croatian**, became prime minister of **Yugoslavia** in January 1989, and, in late December, introduced radical economic reforms. His program successfully curbed inflation, and Marković became the most respected Yugoslav leader. He wants to keep the country together and may be the only person capable of preserving the union.

Marxism-Leninism was the term for the ideological package that several generations of children and adults in the Communist countries were taught in schools and in special seminars. The main pillars of this teaching are:
• All human history until the **October Revolution** was characterized by class struggle.
• The Communist party is the vanguard of the working class.
• The **U.S.S.R.** is the cradle of socialism and the protector of all the oppressed peoples in the world.
• The imperialists, led by the **U.S.**, exploit workers and support all **anti-socialist**, **counterrevolutionary** forces in the world.
• The socialist economy is the only scientific system that has eliminated exploitation of workers.

Mazowiecki, Tadeusz (1927-), a Polish Catholic intellectual and an editor of a Catholic weekly, Mazowiecki was active in the **Solidarity** movement and was picked by **Wałęsa** in August 1989 to become prime minister of **Poland**, the first non-Communist prime minister in **Eastern Europe**. In the summer of 1990, Mazowiecki and **Wałęsa** became opponents. That fall, Mazowiecki lost his bid for the presidency and resigned. Often described as remote and aloof, Mazowiecki is the representative of Polish intellectuals.

Moldavia, the second-smallest Soviet republic, about the size of Massachusetts and Connecticut combined, with just over 4 million people, was annexed to the **U.S.S.R.** in June 1940. The Moldavian language, virtually identical to Romanian, was made a state language in August 1989, a move that provoked opposition from ethnic non-Moldavians, who constitute one-third of the republic's population. In June 1990, Moldavia declared its sovereignty.

Nagorno-Karabakh is a small region within **Azerbaijan**, but three-quarters of its population is Armenian. The first violent conflict took place in February 1988, when the local government requested that Nagorno-Karabakh be transferred to **Armenia**; this led to an anti-Armenian riot in the city of Sugmait in **Azerbaijan** during which 32 people were killed. Since then, there have been numerous other outbursts of violence.

NATO (North Atlantic Treaty Organization) was created in 1949 by a treaty between the **U.S.**, Canada, and 10 West European nations who agreed to join against a common enemy, Communist **U.S.S.R.** and **Eastern**

Throughout the Cold War, NATO stood prepared to deflect a Soviet invasion of Western Europe.

Europe. Several other nations joined later, and, in 1990, the unified Germany also became a member. The enemy has now undergone a transformation, and so NATO plans to redefine its new role in the undivided Europe by the spring of 1991.

Nomenclature is the term designating the high party and state bureaucrats in the Communist systems who were the actual rulers of those countries. After the revolutions of late 1989, the public in Eastern European countries was shocked to see on their television screens the hidden luxuries enjoyed by nomenclature members—from golden faucets in the **Ceaucescus'** villas, to **Honecker**'s sumptuously furnished hunting lodges, to supermodern hotels with deluxe suites exclusively for party members in **Czechoslovakia**.

October Revolution, which actually took place on November 7, 1917 (according to the old Russian calendar), in Petrograd (later renamed Leningrad), was one of the crucial moments of the 20th century. This was the beginning of Soviet history and of modern **Communism**; until the late 1980s, its anniversary was dutifully celebrated in all the Communist capitals around the world. As a sad summation of the "historical significance" of the October Revolution, a banner was carried during the 72nd celebrations in Moscow, saying, "Seventy-Two Years of Going Nowhere."

Perestroika means "restructuring," was introduced by **Mikhail Gorbachev** when he embarked on his road to a thorough transformation of the Soviet economic, political, and social system. Its twin term is **glasnost**, an "openness" about present and past problems. After five years, however,

Liberalized social policies now even permit Western rock bands to perform in the U.S.S.R.

perestroika seems to have brought only disarray, shortages, collapse of authority, and nationalist conflict. **Gorbachev** is increasingly being blamed for all the ills that now beset the **U.S.S.R.**

Personality cult was a distinctive feature of Communist societies. The first and probably the greatest personality cult enveloped **Stalin**, who was elevated to a virtually godlike position and was said to be an over-all genius in practically everything: the wisest of men, the most beloved leader, the greatest war hero, the most brilliant scientist. Streets and cities were named after **Stalin**, and monuments to him dotted most of the Communist world. In **Eastern Europe**, the most pronounced personality cults surrounded **Ceauşescu** of **Romania**, **Tito** of **Yugoslavia**, and Hoxha of **Albania**.

Poland is a flat country in central Europe, about the same size as New Mexico and with a population of 37 million. Poland's history started 1,000 years ago, and, during the Middle Ages, the country was an important central European kingdom. At the end of the 18th century, the so-called "three partitions" erased Poland from the map, its territory being divided between **Russia**, Prussia, and Austria. The Polish nation survived, however, and regained its political independence in 1918, as one of the successor states of the Austro-Hungarian Empire.

The attack on Poland by Nazi Germany was the first act of World War II, and while German armies advanced from the west, Soviet armies entered Poland from the east. Within several weeks, the country was devastated, and the devastation continued throughout the war. Numerous concentration camps were set up on Polish soil, the most infamous of them the extermination camp at Auschwitz where at least 1 million people were killed.

After the war, Poland was "shifted" westward: its eastern part was retained by the **U.S.S.R.**, and, in compensation, the country gained a large territory in the west, which before World War II had belonged to Germany. The Communists took over in 1948, and, in the first period, closely followed the Soviet model. At that time, anti-Soviet resentment, based on historical anti-Russian feelings, was fueled by the presence of a Soviet general of Polish birth in the Polish government. In 1956, shortly after **Khrushchev**'s "secret speech" denouncing **Stalin**, Polish nationalist sentiment combined with economic grievances erupted in workers' riots in the city of Poznań. The riots brought down the Politburo and elevated Władysław Gomułka to the leadership of the party. From then on, the history of Communist Poland was marked by two significant characteristics: continuing workers' unrest and the important role of the church.

Gomułka had been imprisoned for his nationalist leanings after 1949, and when he became the party chief, he introduced a number of liberal reforms, abolished the farm collectivization program, and improved relations with the church. During the 1960s, however, he became more and more rigid, and, in 1968, suppressed a widespread student movement that demanded democratic changes; the leaders of the movement were accused of **antisocialist** activity, and many were forced into exile. The campaign had a clear anti-Semitic character, and about 12,000 Polish Jews left Poland at that time.

Two years later, in December 1970, workers' riots in Gdansk were brutally suppressed, with at least 44 persons killed. Gomułka was forced to resign. He was replaced by Edward Gierek, who quickly became one of the main proponents of **détente** with the West. Gierek traveled to Western capitals and during his tenure, three **U.S.** presidents visited Poland. Gierek also incurred a huge foreign debt, but the borrowed money was not spent wisely, and the economic situation was constantly deteriorating. Workers' riots took place again in 1976. Two years later, however, the Polish nation suddenly had a reason to rejoice when the archbishop of Cracow became Pope **John Paul II**. This event played a crucial, albeit indirect, role in the demise of **Communism** in **Eastern Europe**: it tremendously increased the self-confidence of Poles and gave them courage to challenge their rulers. And so, in August 1980, the famous **Solidarity** was born, and **Lech Wałęsa** became the darling of the international press. This also marked the end of Gierek's political career and the beginning of the decade of **Wojciech Jaruzelski**.

The fifteen months of **Solidarity** ascendancy were a fascinating period, and it almost seemed that Communist rule was coming to an end in Poland. The time was not yet ripe, however, and, in December 1981, **Jaruzelski** declared martial law and abolished all the newly gained freedoms. He could not contain the tide of history, however. **Solidarity** never disappeared, despite the ban. Meanwhile, **Gorbachev** came to power in the **U.S.S.R.**, and the situation changed again.

In the spring of 1989, **Solidarity** was relegalized, and, in the partially free elections of June 1989, it won a resounding victory. The following August, Poland had its first non-Communist prime minister since 1948: **Tadeusz Mazowiecki**, a Catholic intellectual and a close friend

The Roman Catholic Church has helped inspire the Polish people in their struggle against Communism.

and adviser of **Wałęsa**. His government concentrated on economic reform and, in early 1990, introduced radical austerity measures to curb inflation and to set the country on a transition to market economy. In the summer of 1990, there occurred a split within **Solidarity**, which culminated in the presidential contest between **Mazowiecki** and **Wałęsa**. **Wałęsa** won the presidency by a landslide in December 1990.

Prague Spring was a period from early January to August 20, 1968, in **Czechoslovakia**, when, under the leadership of a reformist Communist intelligentsia, and with sometimes reluctant support from a government led by **Alexander Dubček**, the society set on a course of radical liberalization and democratization. The **U.S.S.R.**, led by **Brezhnev**, considered these changes too dangerous, and, in August, crushed the movement with the help of 500,000 **Warsaw Pact** troops. Asked in 1987 about the difference between **Prague Spring** and **glasnost** and **perestroika**, Soviet foreign ministry spokesman Gerasimov replied, "Nineteen years."

Reagan, Ronald (1911-), 40th president of the **U.S.**, from 1981 to 1989. He was elected less than a year after the Soviet invasion of Afghanistan, and, in his first presidential term, called the **U.S.S.R.** "an evil empire." He accelerated the arms race, thus putting additional pressure on the **U.S.S.R.** and indirectly contributing to the deepening crisis of the Soviet system. Two months after Ronald Reagan's second inauguration, **Mikhail Gorbachev** became the general secretary of the **U.S.S.R.**, and, in the fall of 1986, the two leaders met in the first of their four summit meetings.

Revisionism is a term that has been applied by hard-line Communists to various types of reform-minded Communists since the beginning of the 20th century. In 1948, **Tito**'s **Yugoslavia** was branded revisionist and expelled from the Cominform, an international body of Communist countries led by the **U.S.S.R.**; and when **Khrushchev** denounced **Stalin**, **Albania** accused the **U.S.S.R.** of revisionism. In the 1970s and 1980s, the word was largely replaced by the expression **antisocialist**.

Romania is a round-shaped country in the Balkans, bordering on the Black Sea, slightly larger than Utah and slightly smaller than Oregon, with 23 million people. It is the easternmost outpost of a Romance language: Romanian derives from Latin as was spoken in the eastern part of the Roman Empire. Vlado Tepes the Impaler, a medieval Romanian hero who fought the Turks, was popularized in a 19th-century novel and turned into the modern Dracula.

Long under the rule of foreign powers, the present-day Romania began to emerge in the middle of the 19th century. Between the world wars, it was a royal dictatorship, and then it fought on the side of the Germans. In 1944, the Communists took over and, for the next two decades, closely followed the Soviet model.

A new period began in 1965, when **Nicolae Ceauşescu** was elevated to the leadership of Romania. The **Ceauşescu** era was first marked by a more independent foreign policy and an opening to the West, but then increasingly by an accumulation of power by **Ceauşescu** and his family, and a **personality cult** unparalleled in the Communist world since **Stalin**.

In the 1980s, in order to reach his goal of paying off all foreign debt, **Ceauşescu** wreaked untold hardships upon the people. Drastic cuts in energy darkened Romanian apartments and streets, and in winter there was not enough heat. Food was exported, and the people were half-starving. To compound the general bleakness of life, the government introduced the so-called "systematization plan," which called for demolishing up to 7,000 villages and moving people into huge agro-industrial complexes.

The end of the **Ceauşescu** era was a combination of a popular revolt and a coup. It started on December 17, 1989, in the predominantly Hungarian city of Timişoara, when the *Securitate* police and army troops fired into a crowd of people protesting the deportation order served on a Protestant Hungarian pastor, László Tökes. Despite fatalities, the protesting crowds grew larger, and demonstrations spread to other parts of the country. On December 21, **Ceauşescu** addressed a large official rally, during which millions of people around the world watched while he was heckled. Hours later, fighting broke out in the capital, and, the next day

Much death and destruction accompanied the overthrow of Romania's Ceauşescu regime in 1989.

Ceauşescu declared a state of emergency, and the radio announced the "suicide" of the defense minister. Actually, the minister was shot by one of **Ceauşescu**'s bodyguards when he refused to use troops against the crowds; this action persuaded the army to take the side of the revolutionaries. After **Ceauşescu's** execution on December 25, the National Salvation Front (NSF), consisting mostly of former high Communist officials and led by **Ion Iliescu**, emerged as the leading political group and gained popular support by abolishing some of the most hated decrees of the **Ceauşescu** era (such as the "systematization plan").

Unfortunately, the violence did not end with the overthrow of the dictator. In March 1990, opposition groups issued the Timişoara Declaration, demanding that former Communists be banned from public office, and asking for a thorough purge of the bureaucracy. This declaration became the rallying point for anti-NSF demonstrations that started in Bucharest in late April and lasted until the elections in May. The government then bussed in miners to the capital, who beat up the demonstrators, killing seven persons. The confrontation severely undercut the position of the NSF and led to the suspension of economic help from the West.

In addition to political violence, a serious ethnic conflict occurred in March 1990 between Hungarians and Romanians in the town of Tigru Mures: about 2,000 Romanian peasants, armed with axes, knives, and scythes, flocked into town and attacked a crowd of 5,000 Hungarians; five people were killed and about 270 injured.

Meanwhile, the first free Romanian elections since 1937 took place in May 1990, with 82 registered political parties. The major ones, apart from the NSF, were led by exiles, and most were immature and badly organized. The extreme repression under **Ceauşescu** (when even type-writers had to be registered) prevented the rise of a strong intellectual middle class that would have been the natural starting point for new political parties. It was therefore no surprise that the NSF won an overwhelming victory, with 66 percent of the vote for the National Assembly and 85 percent of the vote for the NSF presidential candidate, **Ion Iliescu**. But the anti-Communist mood was gaining momentum during the summer, partly due to economic deprivations, and nationwide antigovernment protests and strikes became the order of the day.

Russia, or the Russian Soviet Federal Socialist Republic (RSFSR), is the largest of the Soviet constituent republics, stretching from **Eastern Europe** to the Pacific, and almost the same size as the whole of South America, with a population of 144 million. In May 1990, **Boris Yeltsin** became president of the Russian Federation, and the following month, its parliament declared the republic a sovereign state.

Sakharov, Andrei (1921-89), the father of the Soviet H-bomb, became in 1953 the youngest-ever member of the Soviet Academy of Sciences. In the early 1960s, he began to challenge Soviet authorities, and warned that the division of the world into socialist and capitalist camps presented a mortal danger for all of humanity. He supported Soviet **dissident** writers and the reformers of **Prague Spring**, and his human-rights activities earned him the Nobel Peace Prize in 1975.

After Sakharov sharply criticized the Soviet invasion of Afghanistan in December 1979, he was exiled to the town of Gorki in January 1980. He did not remain silent, although his communication with the outside world became ever more difficult. One day in December 1986, a telephone was suddenly installed in Sakharov's apartment in Gorki, and the next day a personal call from **Gorbachev** summoned the exiled **dissident** to Moscow. It was an event without precedent in Soviet history. In April 1989, Sakharov was elected to the Congress of People's Deputies, but he died of a heart attack in December.

Serbia is the largest of the six republics comprising **Yugoslavia**. Serbs are a Slavic people who for centuries had been under Ottoman rule; they are predominantly Orthodox Christians, and their language is written in the Cyrillic script. In the nationalist conflicts raging in **Yugoslavia**, Serbia wants to strengthen the federal government, but other republics charge that this is intended only to assure Serbian dominance over the other republics.

The hard-line nationalist leader of the Communist Party (which changed its name to the Serbian Socialist Party in 1990), Slobodan Milosević, is generally blamed for the violent ethnic conflict in the province of **Kosovo**.

Sinatra Doctrine. On October 25, 1989, Soviet Foreign Ministry spokesman Gennady Gerasimov said on **U.S.** television that the new **Warsaw Pact** doctrine could now be called the "Sinatra Doctrine," after the famous Frank Sinatra song "I Did It My Way." From now on, Gerasimov implied, all countries in the pact can "do it their way." The Sinatra Doctrine replaced the much more ominous **Brezhnev Doctrine.**

Slovakia is the eastern half of **Czechoslovakia**; it is inhabited by Slovaks. Slovaks and Czechs are both Western Slav peoples, and speak very similar languages, but their relations have been strained. For a thousand years, Slovakia was part of **Hungary** and the only brief period of Slovak political independence came during World War II, when **Slovakia** became a puppet Nazi state. Although Slovaks have no strong, explicit cause for grievances, they raised a huge cry for independence in 1990.

Slovenia, one of the six constituent republics of **Yugoslavia**, lies in the northeastern part of the country, bordering on Austria. It is the richest and the most European of all the Yugoslav republics, and is sometimes compared to **Lithuania** in the **U.S.S.R.** In the first free elections since World War II, in the spring of 1990, a non-Communist coalition called DEMOS won over the Communists, and, in July, **Slovenia** proclaimed its sovereignty.

Socialism, a word that dates from the early 19th century, has been one of the most abused and misused political terms of the 20th century. It has many meanings: when **Stalin** built his "socialism in one country," the system he had in mind was a society totally controlled by him, with much emphasis on heavy industry, forced labor by prisoners, and merciless struggle against the "class enemy." **Dubček**'s "socialism with a human face" was a much more benevolent system, in which the Communist Party would still rule, but in consultation with other groups in society. Yet another kind is the socialism of western social democratic parties, which advocate the modern-day "welfare state."

Solidarity, an independent trade union in **Poland**, was the major protagonist in the last decade of Eastern European **Communism**. On August 14, 1981, an unemployed electrician named **Lech Wałęsa** began to lead a 17-day occupation strike that resulted in the formation of the Solidarity trade union. The union soon claimed a membership of 10 million, and the Communist leadership was forced to legalize Solidarity, and even negotiate with it, often with church officials acting as mediators. During the next 15 months, Solidarity's power grew still greater as it evolved into a more political organization, going so far as to demand free elections and a referendum on forming a non-Communist government. Finally, on December 13, 1981, under tremendous pressure from the **U.S.S.R.** (still firmly ruled by **Brezhnev** and his conservative Politburo), Polish Prime Minister **Wojciech Jaruzelski** set up the Military Council for National Salvation, declared martial law, arrested Solidarity leaders and activists—more than 10,000 people altogether—and suspended the union.

But the suspension and eventual banning of Solidarity was not the end of the war; it was just one other lost battle. With the absence of Soviet pressure after **Gorbachev** came to power, Solidarity began to reassert itself. In 1989, it was relegalized and participated in the partially free elections for the Polish parliament, winning virtually all available seats. In July 1989, an adviser and friend of **Wałęsa**, **Tadeusz Mazowiecki**, became the first non-Communist prime minister of **Poland**.

With Solidarity united mostly by its opposition to the Communist regime, it was quite natural that once this adversary was gone, the move-

During the 1980s, Solidarity was the most effective anti-Communist organization in Eastern Europe.

ment would split. And indeed, in 1990, Solidarity divided into two broad factions: the right-leaning Center Agreement, led by **Wałęsa**, which advocates the removal of most Communists from positions of responsibility; and the left-leaning Citizens' Movement for Democratic Action, associated with **Mazowiecki** and urban intellectuals.

Solzhenitsyn, Aleksandr (1918-), a leading Soviet **dissident** and a winner of the Nobel Prize for Literature in 1970, was forcibly exiled from the **U.S.S.R.** in early 1974 after he published his *Gulag Archipelago*, one of the most important books of the 20th century for its vivid revelation of the extent and the horrors of the system of prisons and forced-labor camps established under **Stalin**.

Solzhenitsyn settled in Vermont and concentrated on writing his mammoth historical reevaluation of Soviet history. His Soviet citizenship was restored in August 1990, but, as of late 1990, he has not yet decided to go back to the **U.S.S.R.**

Stalin, Joseph (1879-1953), shaped the Soviet system in many ways: he made the **U.S.S.R.** a world superpower (albeit with very shaky foundations), and he substantially contributed to the defeat of Hitler. But at the same time, he inflicted on the people of the **U.S.S.R.** extreme suffering, much of which they still live with today. No one killed as many Communists as he did: during the height of his terror, in the 1930s, it was much safer for a Communist to live in a Western country than in the **U.S.S.R.**

Joseph Stalin (left, in 1945 with U.S. President Truman and British Prime Minister Churchill) gave Soviet Communism its authoritarian nature.

Stalin, although Georgian by birth, was a product of Russian history. He created the modern Stalinist system, which has caused so much damage worldwide, not only because it is brutal and intolerant, but also because it has systematically rewarded the worst human qualities—subservience, lying, lack of initiative, servility, and envy—and punished such qualities as courage, creativity, industriousness, and truthfulness.

Much more devious than Hitler, Stalin duped quite a few Westerners who praised his simplicity and even charm. The **personality cult** elevated him to a godlike position. Despite several decades of **de-Stalinization**, it was only in the late 1980s that the Soviet people began to learn that their beloved dear leader was actually responsible for some 30 million to 50 million deaths.

Tadzhikistan, a Central Asian Soviet republic, about the size of Wisconsin and inhabited by 4.6 million people, was the scene of violent ethnic conflict in February 1990. In August, Tadzhikistan adopted a declaration of sovereignty.

Tito, Josip Broz (1892-1980), born in **Croatia**, was the powerful postwar leader of **Yugoslavia**. He led the Communist guerrillas during World War II, and then took power and remained the paramount chief of the country until his death. Although Tito was an authoritarian ruler, he was not the diabolical dictator of the type of **Stalin** or **Ceauşescu**. He held the country together, balancing traditional national animosities and making **Yugoslavia** a special case of a relatively liberal socialist country.

Ukraine is the second largest constituent republic of the **U.S.S.R.**, twice the size of Arizona and with a population of 50 million. Centering around the ancient city of Kiev, Ukrainians have had a love-hate relationship with Russians for centuries. A nationalist movement, called Rukh, pushed through a declaration of sovereignty in July 1990.

Union of Soviet Socialist Republics (the **U.S.S.R.** or the **Soviet Union** for short). Just the basic statistics are overwhelming: it is the largest country in the world, almost 2.5 times the size of the **U.S.**, stretching from central Europe to the Pacific across 11 time zones, with more than 100 nationalities and 112 officially recognized languages. It is a country of contrasts, and its social and political settings range from **Lithuania**, a very European **Baltic** country in the West, to the Chukchi Siberian groups in the northeast whose lives resemble those of the Canadian Eskimo, and to the Muslim republics of **Uzbekistan**, **Kazakhstan**, **Kirghizia**, and **Tadzhikistan** in Central Asia.

The U.S.S.R. is the heir to the Russian Empire, which had emerged in the 13th century as the little landlocked duchy of Muscovy, and then gradually expanded to roughly its present size. **Russia** traditionally had a complex relationship with Europe, trying during successive periods to emulate European civilization, and yet resisting Western ways.

When the Bolsheviks took over in 1917, in the **October Revolution**, and emerged victorious after three years of civil war, they believed that they started a "world revolution." Instead, their "social experiment" became one of the two greatest tragedies, together with Nazism, of the 20th century.

The Soviet system went through several periods: from the early revolutionary euphoria, to **Stalin**'s terror of the 1930s, to a great patriotic upsurge during World War II, and then to the postwar period of empire building, **Khrushchev**'s **de-Stalinization**, **Brezhnev**'s **détente**, and finally the period of "stagnation" of the 1980s. By then, it was becoming more and more obvious that the system did not work: the U.S.S.R. was a world superpower, with a great arsenal of nuclear weapons and space technology, and yet the average villagers lived almost as they did in the 19th

Residents of the Baltic Republics have voted to secede from the Soviet Union.

*Life in the rural villages of the Soviet Union has
improved little during the 20th century.*

century. In the cities, the time spent standing in queues for everything represented millions of lost hours of work and instilled the people with an overwhelming resentment and dissatisfaction. Nothing seemed to work, and no one seemed to believe in anything anymore; the teachings of **Marxism-Leninism** were just empty formulas repeated automatically when it was required. Alcoholism became a major problem as many men resorted to the ubiquitous Russian vodka to drown their sorrows. The Soviet people were tired, skeptical, and disillusioned, the economy was declining, and the entire society was like an extremely sick patient.

When **Mikhail Gorbachev** took over in March 1985 and embarked on his reform course, he was probably not aware that he was opening a Pandora's box. His **glasnost** and **perestroika** shook the stagnant waters of the system, and at the beginning promised to be the miraculous medicine needed to put the society back into shape. It turned out, however, that the patient was even sicker than he seemed, and while **Gorbachev** was reaping applause throughout the Western world, his own country was getting into deeper and deeper difficulties: growing economic problems, shortages of everything, nationalist conflicts, separatism, and loss of political authority.

Between December 1989 and September 1990, several versions of an economic-reform program were elaborated, always to be rejected either because they were too radical or too slow. By the end of 1990, a mood of national exasperation had taken hold of the country, with real threat of famine in many places, and fears of popular uprising. **Gorbachev**'s popularity reached an all-time low. In November, he unveiled a plan to revamp the government by having the country's main executive body be a council representing individual Soviet republics. Although the plan was initially hailed by the press as the needed energetic action, it was rejected by his main rival, **Boris Yeltsin**, as insufficient.

And so, in late 1990, the U.S.S.R. might be near the breaking point, and whatever is said about the country today may not be true tomorrow. Just look at some of the problems:

- Thirteen out of 15 republics have declared sovereignty, and many want outright independence.
- Violent ethnic conflicts have already caused hundreds of deaths and, with economic decline, are likely to continue.
- **Boris Yeltsin**, the president of **Russia**, is no longer a Communist; he poses the greatest challenge to **Gorbachev**'s rule.
- The mayors of the two largest cities, Moscow and Leningrad, are no longer Communist Party members.
- The hard-liners and conservatives might not be able to unseat **Gorbachev** or other reformers at the top, but they are all-powerful at the lower levels of the bureaucracy.
- Despite declining popularity, **Gorbachev** still enjoys great prestige. His harshest critics realize that at present he is the best representative of the country abroad, even if he is no longer able to enforce his decrees and decisions at home.
- There are shortages of everything, and rationing of basic goods has been introduced in many cities.
- Violent crime has become a major problem, with Leningrad taking first place as the crime capital of the country. The crimes include prostitution, tourist robberies, kidnappings, murders, and black market in arms
- People are leaving the U.S.S.R.: over one-third of a million left during 1988 and 1989, and more than a quarter of a million people left between January and June 1990.
- Military service is still compulsory for all young men, but draft dodging has become common, especially in the **Baltic Republics**.
- Amid all this impending chaos, the U.S.S.R. still possesses enough nuclear weapons to destroy this planet.

These are truly historic times. If the U.S.S.R. survives this winter of discontent and maybe a few more years of difficulties and problems, it could emerge as a new commonwealth of autonomous nations. If that happens, it will be a great victory for the whole world. If not, anything might happen.

United States (or **U.S.**) has fascinated the peoples in the **U.S.S.R.** and in **Eastern Europe** for decades. Despite being violently and continually attacked by official propaganda, it has been admired as a country of jeans, rock and roll, and tall, smiling people with beautiful white teeth. Several generations of Eastern European children have been brought up on adventure books by Karl May, a German who never set foot in America, but wrote a series of novels about the American Indians. The U.S. has also been known from the movies and from the works of such authors as Ernest Hemingway and Kurt Vonnegut, both extremely popular. Even now, with many more personal contacts and the **Cold War** rhetoric gone, the U. S. continues to be a somewhat frightening, mysterious, inscrutable, and tremendously attractive place.

Uzbekistan, twice as big as Utah, is a Central Asian Soviet republic with over 18 million people. In December 1988 and again in December 1989, a number of high Uzbek officials were sentenced for taking bribes and for corruption. Violent conflict took place between Uzbeks and Meshkhetians in the summer of 1989. In June 1990, its Supreme Soviet declared Uzbekistan's sovereignty.

Lech Wałęsa, the first leader of Solidarity (below), was elected president of Poland in 1990.

Wałęsa, Lech (1943-), an electrician with just a high school education, was the leader of **Solidarity** in 1980-81 and the Nobel Peace Prize winner in 1983. His political activism began during the December 1970 strikes in Gdansk; by August 1980, he had become an international celebrity almost overnight. He met with his compatriot Pope **John Paul II** several times, and held discussions with numerous world politicians. In 1987, he published his autobiography, *A Way of Hope*.

During the Cold War, the Warsaw Pact leaders met regularly to discuss mutual defense strategies.

On December 9, 1990, Wałęsa, in a landslide victory, was elected president of **Poland**.

Warsaw Pact. A military alliance formed in 1955 as a response to **NATO**. Its original members were **Albania**, **Bulgaria**, **Czechoslovakia**, **East Germany**, **Hungary**, **Poland**, **Romania**, and the **U.S.S.R.**; **Albania** stopped participating in the alliance in the early 1960s, and formally left it in 1968. The only military action that the Warsaw Pact armies ever took was the invasion of **Czechoslovakia** in August 1968. **Romania** did not participate in the invasion.

In June 1990, the leaders of the Warsaw Pact countries agreed to retain the alliance for a transitional period. **East Germany** formally quit the pact shortly before its reunification with West Germany in October 1990.

Yeltsin, Boris (1931-), a leading Russian radical politician whose career in the late 1980s has provided vivid proof of how things have changed in the **U.S.S.R.** In the fall of 1987, Yeltsin was attacked by **Gorbachev** for his vanity and excessive personal ambition, and then was sacked from the Moscow municipal committee. If **Stalin** had taken a dislike to him, Yeltsin would have paid with his life; under **Brezhnev**, he would have become a "nonperson" (like **Khrushchev**). But under **Gorbachev**, Yeltsin made a spectacular comeback in the spring of 1989, when, in a landslide victory, he was elected to the Congress of People's Deputies.

In June 1990, Yeltsin was elected President of **Russia**, the largest constituent republic of the **U.S.S.R.** The following month, he dramati-

Boris Yeltsin, the president of Russia, may well be the most popular person in the U.S.S.R.

cally announced at the 28th party congress that he was quitting the party, thus inspiring the liberal mayors of Moscow and Leningrad to quit the Communist ranks as well. By the fall of 1990, Yeltsin had become the second-leading politician in the **U.S.S.R.**, vastly more popular than **Gorbachev**. His engaging manner, a mane of white hair, a certain flamboyance, and a great sense of drama make him a darling of the crowds. Yeltsin has been very perceptive in his criticism of Gorbachev, but he still has to prove that he can be a builder as well as a critic.

Yugoslavia is a very old and very young country at the same time. It lies in the Balkan Peninsula on the Adriatic Sea and is about half the size of Kentucky; its population numbers 24 million. A popular description says that Yugoslavia is *one* country with *two* alphabets (Latin and Cyrillic), *three* religions (Catholicism, Eastern Orthodoxy, and Islam), *four* languages (Serbo-Croatian, Slovenian, Macedonian, and Albanian), *five* (principal) nationalities (Serbs, Croats, Slovenians, Macedonians, and Montenegrins), *six* (very quarrelsome) constituent republics (**Serbia**, **Croatia**, **Slovenia**, Bosnia-Herzegovina, Macedonia, and Montenegro), and a border with *seven* countries (Italy, Austria, **Hungary**, **Romania**, **Bulgaria**, Greece, and **Albania**).

Quite a few Yugoslav cities were flourishing during the Roman Empire, but in its present form, Yugoslavia dates from 1918, and the name ("country of southern Slavs") was first used only in 1929. During World War II, **Yugoslavia** was the scene of a fierce guerrilla war between partisans and groups allied with the Fascists; some 1.7 million Yugoslavs were killed. The fighting left deep scars and lingering animosities, especially between the Serbs and the Croats.

When the war ended, the Communists took over, led by the charismatic **Josip Broz Tito**, who held the country firmly together until his death in 1980. **Tito** won great respect both within Yugoslavia and abroad for his defiance vis-à-vis **Stalin** and for his "independent road toward **socialism**." In the 1960s, Yugoslavia became a leading country in the nonaligned movement and also embarked on far-reaching economic reforms.

And thus, for several decades, Yugoslavia balanced on the dividing line between a typical Communist state (it had only one party, with supreme powers; there was press censorship; and people were put in prison for political reasons) and an open liberal society (most Yugoslavs could travel quite freely; there was a lively contact with the West; and, most of the time, political oppression was not very noticeable). When **Tito** died, nationalist tensions began to come to the fore. The hottest point of nationalist conflict since 1988 has been in the province of **Kosovo**.

In late 1989, when the Eastern European Communist regimes collapsed one after another, Yugoslavia felt left behind: ironically, even though for a long time it had been the most liberal of all Communist countries, it was now, at the beginning of 1990, the only state apart from **Albania** where the Communist Party still claimed the leading role. That soon changed, and, in late January, the League of Communists of Yugoslavia practically disintegrated. From that moment, the speed of events accelerated: in **Slovenia** and **Croatia**, non-Communist parties won in the spring elections, and nationalist tensions increased throughout the

Restive nationalist groups have made demonstrations almost a daily occurrence in Yugoslavia.

country. Elections held in **Serbia** in late 1990, however, gave revamped Communists a strong majority. Not surprisingly, then, there is an increasingly hostile relationship between **Serbia** on the one hand and **Croatia** and **Slovenia** on the other hand, with a dispute raging about the future federal system: **Slovenia** and **Croatia** want a loose confederacy, while **Serbia** advocates a strong federal government. Amid all the predictions about imminent disintegration, there is one person who commands great respect throughout the country, and who just might—if he is strong enough and lucky enough—hold the country together: Prime Minister **Ante Marković**. In early 1990, **Marković** tamed runaway inflation and won great praise for his economic reform program.

Zhivkov, Todor (1911-). Leader of the Communist Party in **Bulgaria** from 1954 until his removal in November 1989, Zhivkov had the second longest tenure among the East European leaders, after the Albanian Enver Hoxha. Throughout 1990, there were cries for a trial of Zhivkov and his aides for corruption, abuse of power, and incitement of ethnic hatred, but no formal legal proceedings have been started. In a November 1990 interview, Zhivkov refused responsibility for the establishment of death camps where many thousands of Bulgarians died in the late 1940s and early 1950s. Zhirhor further asserted that Bulgarians lived good lives under his leadership.

*The crowds that brought down the Communist regimes
must now build up strong democratic governments.*

Looking toward
the next century

In early 1990, a great sense of euphoria swept through Europe and
the rest of the world: it seemed unbelievable that the Communist regimes
in Eastern Europe could have fallen so easily. It was exhilarating to see
the formerly prohibited names suddenly all around you: dissidents were
elected presidents, exiles flocked back to their homelands from all over
the world, and each Eastern European country began to rediscover its
history, which had been in so many cases tortured beyond recognition.
All the taboos of the past decades were suddenly broken, and the fear
seemed all gone.

But as time went on, the exhilaration and euphoria began to fade,
and one year after the revolutions, in late 1990, a sense of fatigue, dis-
illusion, and disappointment has become evident throughout the former

Soviet bloc. With a looming economic crisis on the horizon, many people are frightened and insecure, and some talk with nostalgia about the predictability of the previous era.

The main general problem facing each post-Communist country is the replacement of the old nomenclature with new people. It was one thing to depose the leadership, but how do you replace tens of thousands of people in higher political and economic positions? The nomenclature's power was so pervasive that it almost resembled a metastatic cancer spread throughout the whole society. The new rulers want to break the power of the nomenclature without starting a witch-hunt for former Communists.

A related problem is how to learn democratic ways. In Central European countries, it is easier because they all had some democratic experiences in their pasts, but the Balkan countries and the U.S.S.R. had never experienced democracy and do not really know how it works. Few Eastern Europeans know how to "respectfully disagree," and, in their new legislative bodies, they endlessly grapple with procedural questions. After decades of enforced silence and conformity, everyone now wants to be heard, and the result is a cacophony of voices and opinions.

Looking at the immediate post-Communist future from another perspective, the problems can be grouped into four major categories, four E's: Ethnic and nationalist conflicts, Economy, Ecology, and Education.

Ethnic and Nationalist Conflict

The new freedoms brought with them the resurfacing of historical rivalries that had been submerged throughout the Communist period. Unfortunately, Central and Eastern Europeans do not have very friendly feelings toward their immediate neighbors. Poles, Hungarians, and Czechs look down on each other; Slovaks resent both Czechs and Hungarians; Romanians see Hungarians as arrogant and overbearing, and Yugoslavia's nationalities, particularly Serbs and Croats, tend to get into fights over centuries-old wrongs. After the official propaganda relentlessly attacked the United States for racism, the newly free Central and Eastern European societies are now beginning to witness racist violence: attacks on Gypsies and on Vietnamese foreign workers occurred in several countries, and there are signs of anti-Semitism. It is quite probable that some of the racial and nationalist conflict is being fomented by the old members of the nomenclature, who do not have any reason to wish the emerging democratic regimes any luck.

Ethnic and nationalist conflicts are almost everywhere, but there are great differences between individual countries. The following is a quick look at the whole scale.

• The *Soviet Union* is the most extreme case. Far from a melting pot, the country is administratively divided into 15 separate republics, but actually contains over 100 nationalities and ethnic groups. There has been a lot of violence already, between the Armenians and the Azerbaijani, the Georgians and the Abkhas, the Uzbeks and the Meshketians, and the list could go on. Not only individual republics, but also many small regions and districts have already proclaimed their sovereignty, and the central political authority is rapidly declining. The overwhelming question not only for the U.S.S.R. but for the rest of the world is whether the country can stay together. The optimal solution

Long-suppressed bigotries quickly surfaced in the newly liberalized Eastern European societies.

would be a sort of Soviet commonwealth, but many observers feel that this goal is unattainable.

• *Yugoslavia* is next in line: its six republics are at each other's throats, and predictions about an impending disintegration of the country are becoming more frequent. For several years, the most violent place in Yugoslavia has been the province of Kosovo, which is inhabited predominantly by Albanians, but administratively ruled by Serbians. There were also violent conflicts between Serbs and Croats.

• *Czechoslovakia* (renamed *Czech and Slovak Federative Republic* in early 1990) has only two major nationalities, Czechs and Slovaks, but the latter feel very resentful about the alleged Czech dominance and have been pressing for greater autonomy; some groups have even called for Slovak independence.

• *Romania* has a large Hungarian minority of about 2 million. There are deep historical animosities between Hungarians and Romanians, which had soured official Hungarian-Romanian relations even before the upheaval in late 1989. In March 1990, five people were killed in inter-ethnic violence.

• *Bulgaria* has a strong Turkish minority, which had been forcibly assimilated during the 1980s. Anti-Turkish demonstrations took place in early January 1990.

• *Hungary* is very homogeneous within its own borders, but there are large Hungarian minorities in the neighboring countries: 2 million in Romanian Transylvania, about 600,000 in southern Slovakia, and several hundred thousand in the Yugoslav province of Vojvodina.

• *Albania* is quite homogeneous within, but there is a large Albanian minority in the province of Kosovo in Yugoslavia.

• *Poland* is the only country without a serious nationalist problem.

Economy

Economic transformation is the most important goal for the immediate future, but political and nationalist problems complicate and hamper the implementation of radical changes. Almost every Eastern European country tried some sort of economic reform in the last decades of Communist rule, grafting selected free-market principles onto the command-economy system, but all these reforms proved futile, because you cannot have your cake and eat it, too (or, in a pithier expression, you cannot be half-pregnant). It has become generally accepted by the new economic decision makers that nothing but a full-fledged market economy would do. The question is, however, how to introduce it. Where do you start? How fast do you go?

The economic situation at the end of 1990 does not look encouraging. Germany is airlifting emergency food supplies to the Soviet Union, severe food shortages persist in Bulgaria and Romania, formerly East German enterprises are collapsing one after another, about 1 million people are unemployed in Poland, and the oil-price increases are lowering the living standard in both Czechoslovakia and Hungary. Economic performance is down everywhere, and most countries struggle with the problem of privatization. The specter of Soviet economic collapse is frightening because the economies of the formerly Communist countries were so closely tied to the economy of their Big Brother.

Most Eastern Europeans would like to attract Western investors, but Western entrepreneurs are cautious: they must first see guarantees that they would make profits. This is another nightmare of the new economic ministers, bank chiefs, and politicians: how to enact new rules of the game. The legislative mess of old and new laws and regulations is endlessly confusing.

Privatization is on almost everyone's lips, but it has not yet been successfully implemented anywhere. How do you privatize the ubiquitous state property—do you sell it; do you issue coupons; do you distribute it among all citizens? If you decide to sell it, how do you arrive at

Eastern European industry will require much revamping to compete in the world marketplace.

the right price? Poland has the most comprehensive plan for privatization, planning to issue "privatization coupons" to all Poles, and thus to turn more than 7,600 state enterprises into private companies; and Czechoslovakia has a three-stage privatization plan, which should start in early 1991.

Ecology

For years, people in Communist countries knew that they were living in an unhealthy environment, but the truth about the ecological damage is much worse than most suspected. There are several large areas of concentrated damage:

• Coal belt in southeastern East Germany, southern Poland, and northern Czechoslovakia. The high-sulfur, low-quality coal called lignite causes air pollution, acid rain, and respiratory diseases.

• The dirty Danube, from Vienna downstream, no longer has blue waters, but has become one of the most polluted rivers in the world.

• The region in northern Transylvania, in Romania, home to two giant chemical plants, is one of the worst ecological disasters in Europe.

• The Aral Sea in the central U.S.S.R. has shrunk in size by 20 percent, and its waters are now so salty that there is no life in them.

Life expectancy went down in Eastern Europe because of all the pollutants in the air and in many food products; the indiscriminate use of pesticides made some meats (such as beef liver) unfit for consumption. According to Western European estimates, it would take decades to bring Eastern European industrial standards to the level common in most developed countries.

Eastern Europe's dreadful environmental situation may take decades to remedy.

Only through well-equipped schools can young Eastern Europeans master today's technology.

Education

Compared to the ethnic, economic, and ecological problems, the needed changes in education seem somewhat less urgent and easier to implement. With Marxism-Leninism dethroned, teachers are now trying to fill the blank spots created by the Communist regimes, but the teachers are themselves the products of Communist education, and are often at a loss as to how and what to teach in the new times. Some educational fields—such as history, economics, and politics—will have to be completely rebuilt, and new textbooks will have to be written. Even the non-political natural sciences will be changed, however, as the whole school system in Central and Eastern Europe breaks out of its isolation from the international educational community. The schools at all levels will need much assistance from the West, including modern equipment, computers, and scientific instruments. Student and scholar exchanges, which are already developing with most Eastern European countries, will be another important part of the educational renaissance. And so the children of today will be the first generation after many decades that will be taught in free, democratic schools. In them lies the hope for the future.

There is no doubt that the forthcoming years will be full of hardships, struggle, and pain. With the economic disruptions and open borders, millions of people will likely flock to the West in search of better livelihoods; meanwhile, the danger of violent chaos in the U.S.S.R. and in Yugoslavia is very real. And yet, in the long term, we can be reasonably optimistic that this transitional period will gradually pass, and that democratic regimes will replace the old Communist ones.

And so, as we leave the tumultuous and often tragic 20th century, we can look ahead with expectations that, in the opening century of the third millennium, the world will no longer be divided into two hostile camps and that there will be less bloodshed, fewer wars, and more peace and understanding among the peoples on this earth.

INDEX

ILLUSTRATION CREDITS

The following list acknowledges, according to page, the sources of illustrations used in the LANDS AND PEOPLES SPECIAL EDITION: UPHEAVAL IN EUROPE. The credits are listed illustration by illustration—top to bottom, left to right. When the name of the photographer has been listed with the source, the two are separated by a slash. If two or more illustrations appear on the same page, their credits are separated by semicolons.

2	© Robert Wallis/Sipa	44	© Laski/Sipa
7	UPI	46	© Sham Doherty/Liaison
8	UPI	47	UPI
9	Keystone	48	© Patrick Forestier/Sygma
10	© Filip Horvat/Saba	50	© William Stevens/Gamma-Liaison
11	Jose Nicolas/Sipa	51	© V. Kiselyov/Lehtikuva/Woodfin
13	© Thierry Chesnot/Sipa		Camp & Assoc.
16	UPI; © Erich Lessing/Magnum; UPI	52	© Luis Villota/The Stock Market
17	International News Photos	54	© Frederico Mendes/Sipa
18	Paris Match; AP/Wide World Photos	56	Zentrabild
19	UPI	57	© Orban/Sygma
20	UPI; UPI	59	© A. Nogues/Sygma
21	Sygma; UPI; © Keler/Sygma	60	© Chesnot/Sipa;
22	© Roland Neveu/Gamma-Liaison;		AP/Wide World Photos
	AP/Wide World Photos	62	© Shepard Sherbell/Saba
23	UPI; © Ed Wojtas;	63	© Blanche/Gamma-Liaison
	© David Burnett/Contact	64	© Thierry Chesnot/Sipa
24	AP/Wide World Photos	65	© T. Veermae/Lehtikuva/Saba
26	© Laski/Sipa;	67	© P. Robert/Sipa
	AP/Wide World Photos	68	© Le Segretain/Sipa
27	© Kok/Gamma-Liaison	70	© Jurgen Vogt/The Image Bank
28	AP/Wide World Photos	72	© Luc Delahaye/Sipa
30	© Yankelevitch/Sipa	75	© B. Bisson/Sygma
31	© Sygma	76	Signal Corps/Acme
33	© Shepard Sherbell/Saba;	77	© Kimmo Raisanen/Lehtikuva/
	© D. Hudson/Sygma		Woodfin Camp & Assoc.
34	© Witt/Sipa	78	© A. Boulat/Sipa
35	© Luc Delahaye/Sipa;	80	© Alain Dejean/Sygma;
	AP/Wide World Photos		© Chesnot/Laski/Sipa
37	© A. Nogues/Sygma	81	© Laski/Sipa
38	© Alexandra Avakian/Woodfin	83	© Stuart Nichol/Woodfin
	Camp and Assoc.		Camp & Assoc.
39	© Frederic Stevens/Sipa	84	© Van Morvan/Sygma
40	© J. Langevin/Sygma	86	© R. Bossu/Sygma
41	© Chip Hires/Gamma-Liaison;	87	© Christian Valdes/Lehtikuva Oy/Saba
	© Wojtek Laski/Sipa	88	© Dorigny/REA/Saba
42	© Francois Lehr/Sipa	89	© Filip Horvat/Saba

Cover and title page photo: © Avakian/Woodfin Camp & Assoc.
Contents page photos: UPI; © Sygma; © B. Bisson/Sygma; © Van Morvan/Sygma